LITERACY PLAY FOR THE E

Book 2

Learning through non-fiction

COLLETTE DRIFTE

David Fulton Publishers

London

David Fulton Publishers Ltd
The Chiswick Centre, 414 Chiswick High Road, London W4 5TF

www.fultonpublishers.co.uk

First published in Great Britain by David Fulton Publishers 2003
10 9 8 7 6 5 4 3 2 1

Note: the right of Collette Drifte to be identified as the author of this work has been asserted by her in accordance with the Copyright, Designs and Patents Act 1988.

British Library Cataloguing in Publication Data
A catalogue record for this book is available from the British Library.

ISBN 1-85346-957-2

Also available in the **Literacy Play for the Early Years** series:

Book 1: *Learning through fiction* ISBN 1-85346-956-4
Book 3: *Learning through poetry* ISBN 1-85346-958-0
Book 4: *Learning through phonics* ISBN 1-85346-959-9

Cover design by Phil Barker
Designed and typeset by FiSH Books, London
Printed and bound in Great Britain by Thanet Press

Contents

Acknowledgements

The author and publishers would like to thank the copyright holders of the following texts used in this book:

Eyes, Nose, Fingers and Toes by Judy Hindley (Walker Books 1999)
Guess what I am (Walker Books 2000)
My first animal book (Dorling Kindersley 2002)
Dear Zoo by Rod Campbell (Puffin Books 1982)
Is that a butterfly? by Claire Llewellyn (Macmillan Children's Books 2002)
The Very Hungry Caterpillar by Eric Carle (Hamish Hamilton 1994)
What's under the bed? by Mick Manning and Brita Granström (Franklin Watts 1996)
How Do Your Senses Work? by Judy Tatchell (Usborne Publishing 1997)
Homes and Houses Then and Now by Alastair Smith (Usborne Publishing 1999)
Once There Were Giants by Martin Waddell (Walker Books 1989)
My Family Tree Book by Catherine Bruzzone (B Small Publishing 1996)
Travel and Transport Then and Now by Alastair Smith (Usborne Publishing 2000)
Wheels Keep Turning by Mick Manning and Brita Granström (Franklin Watts 2002)

I should like to thank the following for their support and encouragement throughout the writing of this book: Helen Fairlie of David Fulton Publishers for her sound suggestions and professional friendliness; Alan Worth, also of David Fulton Publishers, for seeing the book through the production process; Sophie Cox for her excellent copy-editing; friends and professionals who tried out the activities and made suggestions; the children's parents; and, finally, but probably most important of all, the children themselves. Some of them feature in the little scenarios but, for reasons of confidentiality, their names and details have been altered.

Collette Drifte

For Andrew and Daniel Frampton

Introduction

Curriculum guidance for the foundation stage, the *National Literacy Strategy* and learning through play

Many early years practitioners find it difficult to reconcile the Early learning goals of the foundation stage and the objectives of the *National Literacy Strategy* (DfEE 1998). The philosophy of learning through play is emphasised in *Curriculum guidance for the foundation stage* (DfEE 2000) and rightly so – it is beyond question that young children learn both more, and more effectively, through involvement in activities that are enjoyable, fun, and contain an element of play. The *National Literacy Strategy* (NLS) document outlines its objectives without touching on this in any depth and the practitioner may perhaps feel that it is a sterile document in terms of addressing the concept of learning through play. But the two documents aren't mutually exclusive and they can live alongside each other fairly well, since many of the NLS objectives do actually tie in with the Early learning goals.

For example:

Early learning goals from *Curriculum guidance for the foundation stage*, Communication, language and literacy:

- Enjoy listening to and using spoken and written language, and readily turn to it in their play and learning.
- Use language to imagine and recreate roles and experiences.

Objectives from the *National Literacy Strategy (YR)*:

- To understand and use correctly terms about books and print.
- To use knowledge of familiar texts to re-enact or retell to others, recounting the main points in the correct sequence.

Teresa, the practitioner, Charlie, Nicola, Imogen and Oliver have been looking at a book called *Learning About My Body* by Jo Ellen Moore (Evan-Moor Educational Publishers 2000). They are playing with a plastic skeleton and are busy matching the various body parts with the bones of the skeleton.

> Teresa (pointing to the skull): *What's this?*
> Imogen: *The head – that's the head.*
> Charlie: *It's called the skull. My daddy said it's a skull, the bones in your head.*
> Teresa: *That's right Charlie. Do you know the names of any other bones?*
> Charlie: *Spine. In the book it said your backbone is called your spine.*
> Nicola: *Your ribs – they're in your chest, aren't they Mrs Davies?*
> Teresa: *Yes, that's right, Nicola. Good girl for remembering that. So what are you going to play now?*

The children suggested different games all at the same time, but eventually agreed together to play hospitals and X-rays. In this scenario, the foundation stage goals and NLS objectives listed above have been achieved.

Advisers and inspectors are recommending that early years practitioners give priority to the *Curriculum guidance for the foundation stage* in their setting, so the children should not lose out on either the stepping stones or the learning through play philosophy. As long as you plan your activities within the framework of *Curriculum guidance for the foundation stage*, you will still be addressing many of the NLS objectives when targeting the Early learning goals.

Some professionals working at the foundation stage, however, feel pressurised to teach towards the goals themselves, and are concerned that the stepping stones become overlooked. It is crucial that each child works at an appropriate level and is not pushed ahead too soon towards future outcomes. As professionals, therefore, we need to stand firm in our approach to working with all children at their own level, in their own time. By recording their achievements and showing why they are working on the current stepping stone, we will be able to illustrate the positive reasons for doing this.

Planned activities and appropriate intervention

A second debate to come out of the *Curriculum guidance for the foundation stage* is the principle it promotes of 'activities planned by adults' and 'appropriate intervention' to help the children in their learning (DfEE 2000: 11). Some practitioners feel that children should be left to learn through play, without any intervention by adults, while others may find themselves heavily directing the children's activities in order to highlight a learning point.

Most practitioners, though, would agree that the ideal is a balance between these two and the skill comes in knowing when and how to intervene, to maximise the children's learning opportunity. Leaving children to play freely in the belief that they will eventually learn the targeted skill or concept through discovery, assumes that learning is a sort of process of osmosis by which knowledge is automatically absorbed. This takes learning through play to a questionable extreme and will end up throwing the baby out with the bathwater – a child can play freely all day long without actually coming around to the learning point that the practitioner is aiming for. On the other hand, intervention can easily become interference – it can stifle children's exuberance and enthusiasm for the activity, because their curiosity and creativity are hampered by too much direction from the adult. This will never lead to effective learning. The practitioner needs to be sensitive as to when and how to intervene in the children's play, to help them discover the learning point.

In her book *Understanding Children's Play* (Nelson Thornes 2001), Jennie Lindon outlines the different roles that the professional plays when interacting with the child, including, for example, play companion, model, mediator, facilitator, observer-learner, etc. If you come to recognise which of these roles is appropriate to adopt in a given situation, you will go a long way to making sure children's learning is positive and successful, and fun. The skill lies in ensuring that structure and intervention are there in your planning, which in turn allows the children to determine the nature of the play.

Working towards literacy

When working to develop children's literacy skills, we need to bear in mind that literacy is not confined to reading and writing. All aspects of language as a whole, including speaking, listening, comprehension, expression and conversational skills, are crucial components of literacy. Without language, literacy skills can't be learnt. Speaking and listening feature largely in the *Curriculum guidance for the foundation stage* and so are acknowledged as the fundamental basis of the acquisition of literacy skills. While self-analysis and consideration of others' opinions are featured as objectives at a later stage of the *National Literacy Strategy*, children in the Early Years need to be introduced to these concepts. Paying attention to and taking account of others' views is part of the foundation stage work. Very young children have differing opinions as much as adults and older children, and they need to realise that opinions which are different from their own deserve to be respected and valued.

The reverse of this coin is that they should be able to develop the confidence to express their own opinion in the knowledge that it will be seen as a valuable contribution to the discussions held by the whole group. They must know that even if their opinion is different from others', it is a valid one and will be welcomed by everyone as an alternative view.

Imaginative play, creativity and role-play are also important elements in language development, and therefore in acquiring literacy skills. If we enable children to explore and play in imaginative situations, their ability to understand and enjoy fiction will be enhanced, as will their own creative literary abilities. Fiction and stories are, after all, only a different medium for expressing the creative play that goes on in every early years Home Corner!

Literacy (and language), as such, is not an isolated bubble or a 'subject' of the curriculum to be taught at specific times of the day. It cuts across every area of learning and is part of everything we do. While it is convenient for the sake of record keeping and planning to talk about 'Literacy', it's really something that can't be pigeon-holed or put onto a form with tick-boxes to record when we have 'done' it. It permeates every part of learning: reading the labels on maths equipment together may happen during a maths session, but it's still literacy; writing captions on the bottom of a painting links art and literacy.

So it soon becomes clear how using play, games and fun activities are ways we can approach literacy, enabling the children to develop the skills they need.

Who is this book for?

I hope that all early years practitioners will find something useful in this book and by 'all practitioners', I mean professionals who work in any capacity within the field of early years education. I have tried to use 'neutral' language in the book, i.e. not school-based terms, since the education of early years children takes place in many settings other than schools or nominated educational establishments. Although I have explored some of the issues involved in the *Curriculum guidance for the foundation stage/National Literacy Strategy* debate, this is not to say the implications are only for schools. I would argue that they affect everyone providing education for young children and so the issues are just as relevant to non-school settings.

But aside from this, I hope that the book will be useful to practitioners thanks to the practical nature of the ideas and suggestions. The activities can be done either within the framework of a session aiming for one of the official curriculum targets, or as a non-curriculum session with the setting's own aims in view. Of course, the activities are only suggestions, and practitioners could easily adapt or change them to suit their own situation.

What's in the book?

This book explores a variety of non-fiction texts and how they can be used as the basis of activities that are fun and contain an element of play in them, yet still have a literacy skill as the target. There are new titles and old favourites included in the book. I make no apology for using some of the old favourites since there are always new practitioners and new children entering early years settings, who will discover these delightful books for the first time. The veterans of the game will know that the children who are familiar with the texts never tire of hearing them over and over again, often knowing them word for word!

There are two observation and assessment sections at the end of the book to give the practitioner an idea of what to look for when the children are working to acquire a specific skill. These sections are by no means exhaustive and practitioners can 'pick and mix' the elements that are most useful to them, adding anything that they may feel needs to be included. I can't stress enough the importance of observation as a tool for assessment, since so much can be gathered of a child's achievements, progress and performance by this simple but extremely effective practice. The stepping stones in the *Curriculum guidance for the foundation stage* can also provide a useful guide to the child's achievements, particularly as the colour bands help to put the stepping stones into an age-related context. But we need to remember that they are just that – a guide to the child's progress en route to the Early learning goals – and not be tempted to use them as an assessment or teaching tool as such.

There are also some photocopiable pages which are linked in with the activities. They are not worksheets to be given to the children to 'do', but are a resource to save the practitioner preparation time. They must be used by the adult and the children working together on the activity, in a fun way without pressure.

What's in a chapter?

Each chapter follows the same format:

- Featured text – the title, author and edition used.
- Text synopsis – a brief outline of the book(s).
- Early learning goals from *Curriculum guidance for the foundation stage*, which are relevant to the chapter's focus.
- Objectives from the *National Literacy Strategy*, which link in with the Early learning goals.
- Materials needed – everything needed to do the session and activities.
- Optional materials for other activities – a list of resources needed for the other structured play activities.
- Preparation – details of what needs to be done beforehand. This often includes something like *Make a set of picture matching cards using Photocopiable Sheet 5*. The most effective way of doing this is to photocopy the sheet, stick it onto card and when the glue is dry, cut the sheet into the individual cards. You might like to ask the children to colour those cards that have pictures. You could laminate the cards for future use and to protect against everyday wear and tear.
- Introducing the text – for you as the practitioner either with everyone together or in groups, as you require. Although this section has been scripted, this is for guidance only and naturally you should present the material in your own 'style'. There may be questions asked and issues explored in this section which you feel aren't appropriate for your children's achievement level. The flexibility of the session means that you can 'pick and mix' those bits that *are* relevant to your own situation, leaving out what you don't want, or exploring further something that may be looked at in less detail than you'd like. There may be times when you prefer to explore a text together over several sessions and therefore you might only use part of this section each time.
- Focus activities – these can be done in whichever way you prefer, e.g. adult-led, in groups, independent, child-selected, etc. They have been designed to cater for different achievement levels and obviously you should 'pick and mix' as you require. You could adapt, add to or ignore them according to your own setting's needs. Some of the games have a competitive element in them, for example by winning tokens or avoiding 'elimination'. These can be

adapted, if you prefer, to leave out that element of the game, in which case the children's satisfaction at their own achievement is the outcome of the activity.

- Other structured play activities – suggestions for other things to do as an 'optional extra'. They bring in wider aspects of Early learning goals and the NLS objectives, beyond the chapter's main focus. Some of the activities are competitive but, as mentioned above, you can adapt them to leave out this element if you prefer.
- Related photocopiable sheets.

CHAPTER 1

Eyes, Nose, Fingers and Toes

by Judy Hindley (Walker Books 1999)

Text synopsis

The book is a lively introduction to the various parts of our bodies. It has a text that is fun to read and share, with the opportunity to do accompanying actions. The illustrations are bright and amusing, and offer lots of opportunities for discussion.

Early learning goals from *Curriculum guidance for the foundation stage*, Communication, language and literacy:

- Enjoy listening to and using spoken and written language, and readily turn to it in their play and learning.
- Show...how information can be found in non-fiction texts to answer questions about where, who, why and how.
- Write their own names and other things such as labels and captions...

Objectives from the *National Literacy Strategy (YR)*:

- To understand that words can be written down to be read again for a wide range of purposes.
- To reread a variety of familiar texts, e.g....information books, captions, own and other children's writing.
- To use writing to communicate in a variety of ways... e.g. recounting their own experiences...

Materials needed

- *Eyes, Nose, Fingers and Toes* by Judy Hindley (Walker Books 1999)
- Flip chart and marker pens, Body Chart (see 'Preparation'), large sheet of card, coloured marker pens, pictures of eye, ear, nose, mouth, arms, hands, legs, feet and torso, easel, scissors, glue

- A variety of items for hearing and speaking (e.g. a telephone, a radio, a cassette player and blank cassette, some musical instruments, etc.)
- Body part cards (see 'Preparation'), card
- A selection of small games equipment (e.g. beanbags, quoits, bat and ball, hoops, skittles, etc.). Alternatively, a selection of table-top activities such as threading, weaving, jigsaws, form boards, etc.
- A selection of foods with different flavours and textures (e.g. cheese, jelly, biscuits (sweet and savoury), a variety of fruits and vegetables, etc.). Make sure none of the children is allergic to any of the foods
- Body part pictures (see 'Preparation')

Optional materials for other activities

- Body Chart (see 'Preparation')
- Toy animals or pictures of animals
- *Bobby Shaftoe, clap your hands* by Sue Nicholls (A & C Black 1992)
- Dolls and puppets
- The suggestions on the flip chart from the introductory session

Preparation

▲ Use Photocopiable Sheets 1 and 2 (pp. 11 and 12) to make some body part cards for Group B. Make extra copies of the sheets for each child in Group E.

▲ Make a Body Chart as shown in Figure 1.1 (p. 10) with the pictures and/or labels of the body parts across the top axis and the activities down the side axis. You might include *eating, sleeping, breathing, running, singing* and *playing*. You could put a picture of each activity beside its label. (If you wanted to make alternative versions of a Body Chart, you could use an acetate sheet fixed over the grid, to allow changes of activity and equipment on the side axis.) Put the chart on the easel beside the flip chart.

▲ Prepare the food selection as necessary – let the children help in the preparation.

▲ Cut the photocopiable sheets into the separate pictures for Group E. (Alternatively, let the children cut them up.)

Note: This project may raise issues such as race, disability and so on. Be sensitive to the feelings of the children, particularly those who are personally affected. Use the opportunity to discuss positively and openly any general aspects of these issues that the children may ask about, without focusing on the situation of individual children. If a child makes a disclosure that you are worried about, inform the member of staff who is responsible for child protection matters immediately.

Introducing the text

You may choose to introduce the text over several sessions:

- Show the cover of the book to the children and ask them to read the title with you – can they guess what the book is about? Explain that you're all going to talk about the different parts of our bodies and why we have them. Share the book with the children, encouraging them to join in. When you have finished reading, ask the children whether they enjoyed the book. Can they tell you why or why not? Look through the book again and together, decide on some actions to go with each page of the text. Reread the book, encouraging them to perform their actions as you read.

- Explore the text in more detail. Look at each part of the body and discuss what other jobs they do, as well as those given in the book. Write the children's suggestions on the flip chart. Some ideas they may come up with are:
  - (a) eyes – crying, closing against the wind or rain or specks of dust, opening wide when we're laughing or surprised or scared, closing when we're playing 'Hide and Seek' or waiting for a surprise;
  - (b) nose – breathing, wrinkling, rubbing with the nose of someone we love, rubbing with our hands when we're thinking;
  - (c) ears – hearing other sounds and noises, listening to music, the television, radio and songs;
  - (d) mouth, teeth and tongue – eating and breathing, tasting, chewing, crying, swallowing, licking lollipops, sucking sweets;
  - (e) lips – talking, eating, screwing up when we're unhappy, crying;
  - (f) necks and shoulders – holding our heads and arms in place, necks lead down to our tummies and lungs;
  - (g) backs – lying down, giving piggybacks, carrying rucksacks;
  - (h) arms and hands, fingers and thumbs – holding, catching, throwing, writing, painting, cutting, waving, cuddling;
  - (i) toes, legs and knees – walking, running, swimming, climbing.
- Have a look at the Body Chart with the children and discuss one of the activities in the side axis – can they tell you which body parts are used during the activity? Let them come and put a tick in the appropriate boxes – show them how to find the box by moving from both axes. For example, for eating, they would tick the eyes, mouth, arms and hands boxes. Tell the children they'll have the chance to put more ticks in the right boxes when they do some of the activities later on.
- Spend some time discussing with the children *why* the different parts of our bodies do these jobs. For example, we need to eat, breathe, exercise and sleep to keep well; we need to see, hear and move to keep safe; we need to do all these things to learn about our world and to make relationships. Help them to understand that our overall health and well-being depend on these vital functions.
- Depending on achievement level, you could explore some of the body's systems in a little more detail. For example, read *A nose is to sniff* on the third page of *Eyes, Nose, Fingers and Toes* and ask the children where the sniff goes to, then explain that noses are joined to lungs in our chests; or talk about when we use our mouths for eating and ask where the food goes to, before explaining how our mouths are connected to our stomachs. Does anyone know that the brain tells all our body parts what to do?
- Do some comparisons between the children. For example, explore different eye and hair colourings, heights and weights, eye and nose shapes, hand sizes and spans, skin colours, teeth and mouth shapes. Use the discussion as an opportunity to talk about the physical differences between people in a positive way – that we are all different and that we should respect and value each other, regardless of differences.

Focus activities

Group A: Give the children a variety of objects they can use for hearing and let them explore them freely. For example, two children could hold a telephone conversation, another could listen to the radio, a group of them could listen to a cassette recorded by other children, and the rest could play with some musical instruments. Encourage them to discover how they use their ears, eyes, hands and so on when carrying out their activities. Help them to decide which activities on the Body Chart they were doing (*playing*, *breathing* and possibly *singing*) and to tick the appropriate boxes.

Group B: Put the body cards face down on the table and let the children play a game where they take turns to pick a card and look at the picture of the body part. They should then perform an action using the same body part, and the others have to guess which body part it is. If the children guess body parts that are also used in the mimed action, but that are different from the picture on the card, tell them they are not 'wrong' and praise them for thinking of all possibilities for their answer.

Group C: Let the children experiment with the small games equipment and/or table-top activities. Encourage them to focus on what they're doing and identify which body parts they use while they are doing their activities. For example, if they throw a ball, they use their eyes, arms, hands, fingers and thumbs, legs and feet, back. Help them to decide which activities on the Body Chart they were doing (*playing*, *breathing* and possibly *running*) and to tick the appropriate boxes.

Group D: Let the children have some fun experimenting with the selection of foods. Encourage them to think about the different tastes and textures they experience. Discuss which they like and dislike and why. Help the children to make a record of their conclusions by designing charts. They should all draw ☺ or ☹ beside the name and picture of the items of food they tasted. Can they write a label, caption and/or sentence(s) about their likes and dislikes? Help them to decide which activities on the Body Chart they were doing (*eating*, *playing* and *breathing*) and to tick the appropriate boxes.

Group E: (You may decide to do this activity in a hall, playground or away from the main workroom.) Give the children their body part pictures from Photocopiable Sheets 1 and 2. Play a game where you tell the children to perform an action, such as *run, jump, hop, roll, stretch* and so on. When they have finished, they should hold up the pictures of the body parts they used while doing the action. Which action involved the most body parts to perform?

Other structured play activities

- Encourage the children to think about which parts of their bodies they use when they're playing on the large apparatus, both indoors and outside. Make a new Body Chart where the different pieces of equipment form the side axis. Help the children to find the appropriate boxes and to put ticks in them.
- Look at toy animals or pictures of animals and help the children to label the body parts. Discuss which are different from ours. For example, paws, tails, hooves, manes, horns, antlers, wings and so on. According to achievement level, encourage the children to decide which body parts the animals would use for different activities such as eating, climbing, flying, chasing prey and so on.
- Have fun singing songs that feature body parts. For example: *Heads, shoulders, knees and toes; This is the way we clap our hands (Here we go round the mulberry bush); If you're happy and you know it; Peter taps with one hammer;* and so on. You could record them

onto a cassette and let the children listen and sing in their own time. Use books such as *Bobby Shaftoe, clap your hands* by Sue Nicholls (A & C Black 1992).

- Help the children to make a display of dolls and puppets, with the different body parts labelled.
- Make table displays with objects that emphasise different body parts. For example, for *eyes* you could have a kaleidoscope, binoculars, a telescope, spectacles and sunglasses; for *ears* you could have a radio, a walkman and earphones, a telephone, a hearing aid and some musical instruments.
- Together look at the children's suggestions from the introductory session about the other functions of our body parts (on the flip chart). Have some fun encouraging the children to make up actions to show each one, for example wiping tears from their eyes to show *crying*. Ask the children to draw pictures of the actions and to write a label, caption and/or sentence(s) for their pictures.
- Make available a selection of books about how our bodies work and encourage the children to look at these in their own time.

	eyes	ears	nose	mouth	arms	hands	legs	feet
eating	✓			✓	✓	✓		
sleeping	✓	✓	✓	✓	✓	✓	✓	✓
breathing			✓	✓				
running	✓		✓	✓			✓	✓
singing		✓		✓				
playing	✓	✓	✓	✓	✓	✓	✓	✓

Figure 1.1 An example of a Body Chart

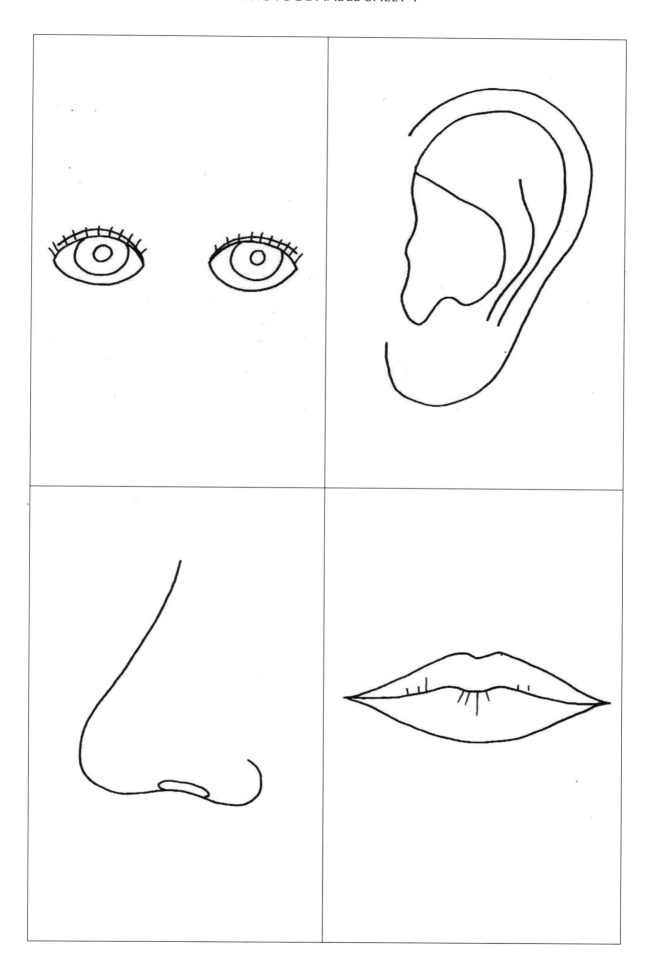

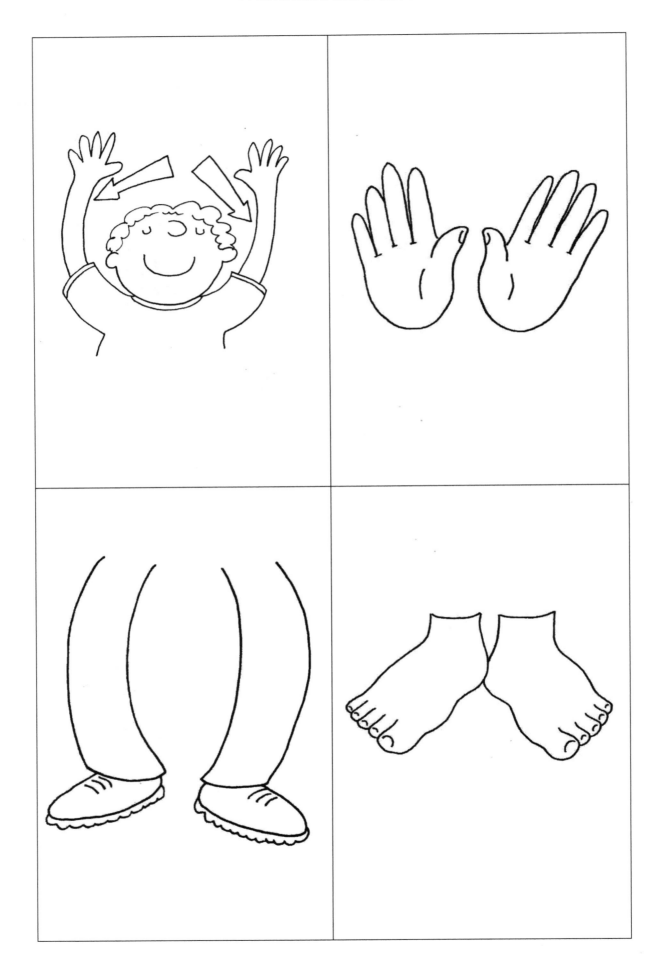

CHAPTER 2

Guess what I am

(Walker Books 2000)

My first animal book

(Dorling Kindersley 2002)

Texts synopses

Guess what I am is a peep-hole book that features wild animals, introduced by their more familiar relations. The reader is invited to guess what the animal is by seeing a small section of a picture and by reading four clues. The book is illustrated with coloured drawings showing each animal in its natural habitat.

    My first animal book has glossy photographs of many animals – wild, domesticated and tame. All the animals featured in *Guess what I am* are also featured in this book, with the exception of the beaver, so the book gives the children the chance to see 'real' pictures of the animals, rather than drawings.

Early learning goals from *Curriculum guidance for the foundation stage*, Communication, language and literacy:

- Extend their vocabulary, exploring the meanings and sounds of new words.
- Use their phonic knowledge to write simple regular words and make phonetically plausible attempts at more complex words.
- Read a range of familiar and common words and simple sentences independently.

Objectives from the *National Literacy Strategy (YR)*:

- To learn new words from their reading and shared experiences.
- To reread frequently a variety of familiar texts, e.g....information books, wall stories, captions, own and other children's writing.
- Through guided and independent writing to write labels or captions for pictures and drawings.
- Through guided and independent writing to write sentences to match pictures or sequences of pictures.

Materials needed

- ■ *Guess what I am* (Walker Books 2000) and *My first animal book* (Dorling Kindersley 2002)
- ■ Paper to make peep-hole books, scissors, pens, coloured marker pens, card
- ■ Animal picture/clue cards (see 'Preparation'), tokens
- ■ Cassette recorder/player and blank cassette
- ■ Mother/baby cards (see 'Preparation')

Optional materials for other activities

- ■ Materials to make masks
- ■ Malleable materials such as plasticine, play dough, etc.
- ■ Materials to make a frieze, including textured materials such as fake fur

Preparation

- ▲ Make a set of animal picture/clue cards using Photocopiable Sheets 3 and 4 (pp. 18 and 19).
- ▲ Record on the blank cassette the following questions and instructions, leaving a long enough pause between each one to allow the children to switch the recorder off and back on again without losing any of the next question:

  What noise does a frog make? Switch off the tape and make the noise.
  What noise does a cricket make? Switch off the tape and make the noise.
  What noise does a dog make? Switch off the tape and make the noise.
  What noise does a bumblebee make? Switch off the tape and make the noise.
  What noise does a brown bear make? Switch off the tape and make the noise.
  What noise does a mouse make? Switch off the tape and make the noise.
  What noise does a lion make? Switch off the tape and make the noise.
  What noise does a canary make? Switch off the tape and make the noise.
  What noise does a snake make? Switch off the tape and make the noise.
  What noise does a duck make? Switch off the tape and make the noise.

- ▲ Make a set of mother/baby cards using Photocopiable Sheets 5 and 6 (pp. 20 and 21).

Introducing the text

You may choose to introduce the text over several sessions:

- Together look at the front cover of *Guess what I am* and ask the children what they think the book might be about. Read the title, encouraging them to join in and ask them whether they think the 'I' of the title means you. Encourage them to guess who 'I' could mean. Can anyone say what *A peep-hole book* might mean?

- Share the book with the children. Read the text slowly, inviting them to guess after each clue what the animal might be, rather than reading all four clues and then asking. Should any of the children make an incorrect but plausible guess from the given clue, praise them for their careful thinking. For example, if *I have wings like this parrot, but I can't fly* leads a child to guess *ostrich* or *emu*, say that the guess was very good for that particular clue, because an ostrich or an emu can't fly, but *ostrich* or *emu* won't fit the next clues. Encourage the children to look for other clues besides those in the text, to help them guess. For example, although the tiger says *This is my long curvy tail*, the children can see that the tail is also striped in orange and black; or although the penguin says only *This is my beak*, the children can see it is pointed and coloured black and orange. Before you turn over each page, spend a few moments talking about the small piece of the picture the children can see through the peep-hole – can they guess what the animal might be from that? After you have turned over each page, and discussed the wild animal, look at the 'tame' animal from the previous page through the peep-hole and then invite the children to read its speech bubble. When you have finished reading the book together, ask the children whether they enjoyed it. Can they tell you why or why not? Which is their favourite animal? Why? Have they ever seen any of the animals in the book? Where? Which is the animal they like the least? Why? Which of the animals they have never seen would they like to see in real life? Why? Is there one of the animals they would never like to come across? Why not?

- Show the cover of *My first animal book* to the children and ask them what they think might be in this book. Explain that among the pictures of all the animals, there are photographs of most of the animals they met in *Guess who I am*. Tell them that while you're all sharing the book, they should try to discover which animal isn't in this book. Take plenty of time to share the book, letting the children savour the photographs. Discuss the animals in terms of: colour (*Who knows what colour this is? Which animal is green? Why is this ladybird red? Who knows what happens to a chameleon's colour?*); size (*Which of these is huge? Is this frog smaller or larger than that frog? Which is the smallest wild cat? Which is the biggest – can you remember from 'Guess who I am?'*); shape (*Which animals have a similar shape to a cat? What shape is a snake? Why is the stick insect/leaf insect/stonefish that shape? Why is an eel long and thin like that?*); texture (*What do you think the puma would feel like if we stroked its fur? How might the porcupine feel if we touched it? What other animal do you know with prickles like that? Would you like to touch the baboon spider? Why or why not?*); and so on. Are there any words that the children aren't sure of? For example, what does *Amazing disguises* mean; or some of the vocabulary in sections such as *Animal movers* (*stalking, strutting, hovering*, etc.)? Explore the specialised sections towards the end of the book and use them to have fun. For example, read the *Animal noises* section and then let the children experiment with voice and body sounds to imitate the animals' noises, or ask them to make up some actions that illustrate the *Animal movers* section. Challenge them to think of a second animal for each colour shown in the *Animal colours* pages. For example, white – lamb, red – ladybird, black – blackbird, and so on. Spend some time looking at *Animal opposites* and then ask the children to think of other things for each set of opposites. If they find it difficult to think of other pairs of animals, let them suggest anything that shows opposites. When you have finished exploring the book, ask the children whether they know which animal is in *Guess what I am* that is not in *My first animal book* (the beaver).

Focus activities

Group A: Use the two books to help the children make their own peep-hole books in the style of *Guess what I am*. Let the children choose several animals from *My first animal book* (the number according to achievement level) and help them to decide on three or four characteristics to use as clues. For example, if they choose a panda, they could give the following clues: *I'm a kind of bear, I'm black and white, I eat bamboo*. Show them how to cut out the peep-holes on alternate pages and then draw their animals with a little bit showing through the hole. You may have to help them write their clues.

Group B: Put the animal picture/clue cards face down on the table and let the children play a game where they take turns to pick a card. They should read the clues to the other children one by one. When another child guesses the animal correctly he or she takes a token, and the card is put back at the bottom of the pile. The winner is the child with the most tokens at the end of the game.

Group C: Give the cassette player and *My first animal book* (open at *Animal noises* on pages 42 and 43) to the children. Ask them to listen to the cassette and follow the instructions. If they need a bit of help, they can look at the book to jog their memories.

Group D: Put the mother/baby cards on the table face down. Let the children play a type of Pelmanism – each child turns over two cards and if they are a mother-baby pair, the child keeps the cards; if not, the cards are turned over again. The winner is the person with the most pairs at the end of the game. Alternatively, the children could play a simple matching game where they pair up the mothers and babies.

Group E: Using the *Animal opposites* page of *My first animal book* as the basis, help the children to draw or paint some of the animals that are featured. The children should write labels, captions and/or sentence(s) to explain about how their animals are opposites.

Other structured play activities

- In the hall or playground, let the children have fun pretending to be some of the animals. Play charades where they have to make the noise and do the actions of a particular animal for the others to guess.
- Make masks of some of the different animals featured in the two books and let the children wear them during their imaginative play.
- Use malleable materials with other things to make models of some of the animals, encouraging the children to think about how they can show the texture of each animal's body. For example, if the children make a porcupine they could use straws for the quills, or if they make a chameleon they could use different pulses for the rough, differently hued skin. The children should write a label, caption and/or sentence(s) about their models.
- Leave both featured books, together with a selection of other books about animals, in the Book Corner, for the children to explore in their own time. If possible, have beanbags and cuddly toys of some of the featured animals in there too, for the children to snuggle while they read.
- Make a large frieze with collages of the animals, using as many differently textured materials as possible. For example, fake fur for the bears or rabbits, painted bubble wrap

for toads or crocodiles and synthetic leather for elephants or rhinoceroses. The children should write labels, captions and/or sentences about the frieze.

- Leave out the cassette player, recorded cassette and *My first animal book* for the children to listen to, make the noises and read in their own time.

I have big sharp teeth
I make dams from logs
I am a beaver

I live in a cold place
I can't fly very well
I am a penguin

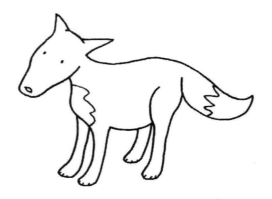

I have big sharp teeth
I swim in the sea
I am a shark

I look like a dog
I have a bushy tail
I am a fox

I am like a cat
I have big sharp teeth
I am a tiger

I am very big
I have a long trunk
I am an elephant

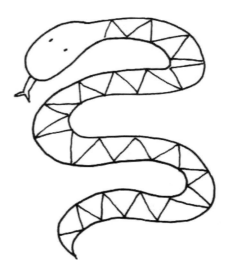

I live up in the trees
I can swing from the branches
I am a monkey

I am long and thin
I make a hissing noise
I am a snake

CHAPTER 3

Dear Zoo

by Rod Campbell (Puffin Books 1982)

Text synopsis

The narrator of the book tells of what happened when they wrote to the zoo asking for a pet. A series of animals arrived, but there was always a reason for not keeping them, and so they were sent back. Until the people at the zoo hit on exactly the right pet – when the basket arrived, what was inside turned out to be perfect.

Early learning goals from *Curriculum guidance for the foundation stage*, Communication, language and literacy:

- Write their own names and other things such as labels and captions and begin to form simple sentences, sometimes using punctuation.
- Use a pencil and hold it effectively to form recognisable letters, most of which are correctly formed.

Objectives from the *National Literacy Strategy (YR)*:

- To use a comfortable and efficient pencil grip; to write letters using the correct sequence of movements.
- To use writing to communicate in a variety of ways, incorporating it into play and everyday classroom life, e.g. . . . greeting cards, letters.

Materials needed

- *Dear Zoo* by Rod Campbell (Puffin Books 1982), flip chart and marker pens (see 'Preparation'), a selection of envelopes and old letters including some from the setting to the parents
- Notepaper, envelopes, stamps, pencils

■ Animal matching cards (see 'Preparation'), card, scissors, glue, Post Office forms, leaflets, etc. (see 'Preparation'), a postbag plus a collection of letters (see 'Preparation'), a post person's hat (optional), a carton (see 'Preparation')

Optional materials for other activities

■ A selection of different envelopes and notepaper
■ Selection of books related to the theme of writing letters, the Post Office, etc.

Preparation

▲ Before you start the project, collect some of the free forms and leaflets that are available from the Post Office.
▲ Divide the second page of the flip chart into six sections and draw an animal from *Dear Zoo* in each one – the drawings don't have to be Michelangelo-standard, as long as they are reasonably identifiable! On the third page, write the setting's address, the date and *Dear . . .* (see Figure 3.1 on p. 27) Cover the pages up.
▲ Using Photocopiable Sheets 7 and 8 (pp. 29 and 30) make a set of animal matching cards.
▲ If possible borrow a postbag, otherwise make one from some red material; fill it with some old letters (the number according to achievement level); make one side of the carton look like a front door, and cut a hole in it for the letterbox.

Introducing the text

You may choose to introduce the text over several sessions:

• Show the front cover of the book to the children and invite them to read the title with you. Can they guess what the book might be about? Share the 'blurb' on the back cover. Ask the children what kind of pet they would like from the zoo, choosing from the animals named on the cover. Can they tell you why? Read the book, inviting the children to join you, and tracking the text with your finger as you read. Before you lift the flap on each page, encourage the children to guess what animal they're going to see underneath. Ask them to give you reasons for their suggestions. Help them to use the clues in the book to decide. For example, by looking at the small part of the animal that might be visible in an illustration, or by reading the label on the animal's container such as *DANGER!* or *VERY HEAVY* and guessing from that. When you have finished reading the book, ask the children whether they enjoyed the story. Can they tell you why or why not? Which animal would they choose if they were the person in the book? Why? Is there an animal they would have sent back to the zoo? Why? Do they think the person in the story made the right choice in the end? Why?

• Look at the text in more detail. Go through the series of animals again and ask the children the reason for each one being sent back to the zoo. For example, the giraffe because he was too tall, or the snake because he was too scary. Do the children agree with these reasons? Can anyone suggest other reasons for sending back each animal? Uncover the pictures on the flip chart and write a few key words for their suggestions in each animal's section. Encourage the children to recount the order in which the animals were delivered to the person in the story.

• Look at the illustrations in the book in more detail. Together read the words on some of the animals' containers and ask the children what they mean. Can they tell you something else that you could use each word for? For example, *fragile* could be used for a box of eggs, or *DANGER!* could be used for a very fast river. Discuss each container and what the children think they might be made from. For example, the lion's cage is probably made with very strong wooden planks and the snake's basket is probably woven from willow or reeds. Can the children suggest why each container is just right for each animal? Why is there a label on some of the containers that says *From the zoo*? Help the children to establish that the animal in its container was sent from the zoo (i.e. not collected by the narrator) and so the zoo people had to identify themselves as the senders.

- Why would the zoo have sent animals in the first place? Reread the opening sentence of the book together – *I wrote to the zoo* – and ask the children what they think this means and what the person in the story wrote. When the discussion comes around to letters and letter writing, hold up some of your selection of letters and explore them together. Who wrote them? Who did they write them to? What about? Point to the address at the top of the paper and ask the children why it is there. Read the opening phrase (*Dear...*), remind the children that the story is called *Dear Zoo* and explain that this is how we usually start a letter. Look at how the letter has been signed off. Explain that we finish a letter in different ways, depending on who it is we're writing to – we would write *Lots of love* at the end of a letter to our Grannies but not in a letter to the bank manager. (Although that might just help when we have an overdraft!) What sort of things might we write in a letter to our Grannies or to a friend who's sick and can't join us for a few days? Show the children the envelopes and ask *What are these called?* (You may well have a difference in pronunciation of the word *envelope*, with some children saying an 'o' sound at the beginning and others saying 'e'.) Can the children tell you what envelopes are for? Point to the addresses and ask the children what they are. Does anyone know why we write the address on the front of envelopes? Can the children tell you their addresses? Invite some of them to come and write their address on the flip chart, or you could scribe it for them. Have a look at the stamps. Ask whose head it is on the stamp. Explain that the Queen's head is on all the stamps in the UK. If you have some children whose family is from a different country, ask whether they can bring in some envelopes with stamps from abroad, so that you can compare them with British stamps.

- Can the children suggest who we might write letters to? Can they say why? For example, to Father Christmas asking for something special, to our friends inviting them to our birthday party or to our Granny because she isn't very well. Can anyone tell you who grown-ups might write to? Explore some of the letters from the setting to the parents and discuss them together. There may be letters, for example, giving information about a Parent/Governors' meeting, about a day trip for the children or about the increased cost of the bus that goes to the swimming baths. What other letters come through the post? For example, electricity, gas or phone bills, brochures and letters from the bank. Have any of the children received letters? Invite them to share their experiences, telling the others who their letters came from and what they were about.

- Look at the page of the flip chart that has the opening of a letter written on it. Talk about the setting's address and its position on the page. Ask the children why you have written the date and what you might write after *Dear*. Together choose someone to write the letter to and why, and encourage the children to decide on its contents. For example, they might choose to write to the Head of the setting inviting him or her to join them for a drink and some cakes the children have made, or to write to the setting's postman, asking him to come and talk to the children about his job. Scribe the letter for the children or, according to achievement level, let them write it themselves.

Focus activities

Group A: Help the children to write a letter to the zoo featured in the book, sending back one of the animals – let them choose which one. They can use the reasons written on the flip chart during the introductory session, or the reason given in *Dear Zoo*. Make a display of their letters, together with illustrations of the animals. Pin the letters at child-eye height so that the other children can read them – a real audience is important to make writing meaningful for the children who write.

Group B: Put one set of the animal matching cards face up on the table. Play a game with the children (or let them play it independently) where they take turns to pick one of the cards from the feely bag, identify the animal on it and match it with the corresponding card on the table.

Group C: Let the children write real letters to someone. Help them to decide who they're going to write to. For example, they could write to another group of children in the setting, telling them how much they enjoyed a performance at assembly given by the other children, or to a member of staff who is away ill. As far as possible, it should be to someone who will write back – you could arrange this beforehand. Let the children look at the letter on the flip chart for support if they wish. They should address the envelope correctly and then stick the stamp in the right place. Organise a trip to the postbox and let the children post their letters themselves.

Group D: Turn the Home Corner into a Post Office. Explore the forms and leaflets that you collected from the real Post Office and discuss with the children what they are for. The children should list and then collect the other things they will need to set up their Post Office, such as envelopes and notepaper, stamps, a few parcels, pension books and so on. Let them role-play in their Post Office during unstructured times.

Group E: Play the Postbag Game with the children. Let them take turns to carry the postbag and wear the hat. Sing *Letters in the postman's bag* (see Figure 3.2 on p. 28) to the tune of *Five Currant Buns*. At the end of each verse, the child delivers the letter through the letterbox in the front door of the carton and then another child takes a turn.

Other structured play activities

- Leave out a selection of different envelopes and writing paper and let the children practise writing letters. You might like to leave out 'samples' of letters for the children to use as models. Make the most of festivals and special occasions to motivate the children in their letter writing. For example, they could write to Father Christmas, the Easter Bunny, or even the Tooth Fairy.
- Ask the children to bring in some old envelopes and letters (with permission) and together make a display. Make a postbox to add to the display and if possible, borrow a postbag to add a touch of realism.
- Ask your setting's post person to come in and talk to the children about his or her job. If possible, arrange a visit by the children to the local Post Office and/or sorting office. Afterwards, help the children to write letters of thanks.
- Leave a selection of books about letters, the postal system and so on for the children to explore in their own time. Some appropriate ones are *Kipper's Birthday* by Mick Inkpen (Hodder Children's Books 1994), *Katie Morag Delivers the Mail* by Mairi Hedderwick

(Red Fox 1997), *The Jolly Postman* by Janet and Allan Ahlberg (Viking Children's Books 1999), *Dear Daddy* by Philippe Dupasquier (Andersen Press 2002), *A Letter to Father Christmas* by Rose Impey and Sue Porter (Orchard Books 2001) and *Tales from Acorn Wood: Postman Bear* by Julia Donaldson (Campbell Books 2000).

Orchard First School
Pear Tree Avenue
Appledale
AD13 8KF
8 April 2003

Dear Katie,

Can you come to a party next week? It is for our teacher's birthday. We will have cakes and fruit juice. The party will be at school on 13 April at 2 o'clock.

Lots of love from

The Children in Cherry Class

Figure 3.1 An example of the beginning of a letter

Letters in the postman's bag Song

Five* special letters in the postman's bag,

Five special letters with a stamp on the front,

Along came Mandeep with the letters one day,

He put one through the door and then he went away.

Four* special letters in the postman's bag,

Four special letters with a stamp on the front,

Along came Suzie with the letters one day,

She put one through the door and then she went away.

* Use the number of letters you think best, according to achievement level.

Figure 3.2 *Letters in the postman's bag* (sung to the tune of *Five Currant Buns*)

lion

lion

monkey

monkey

snake

snake

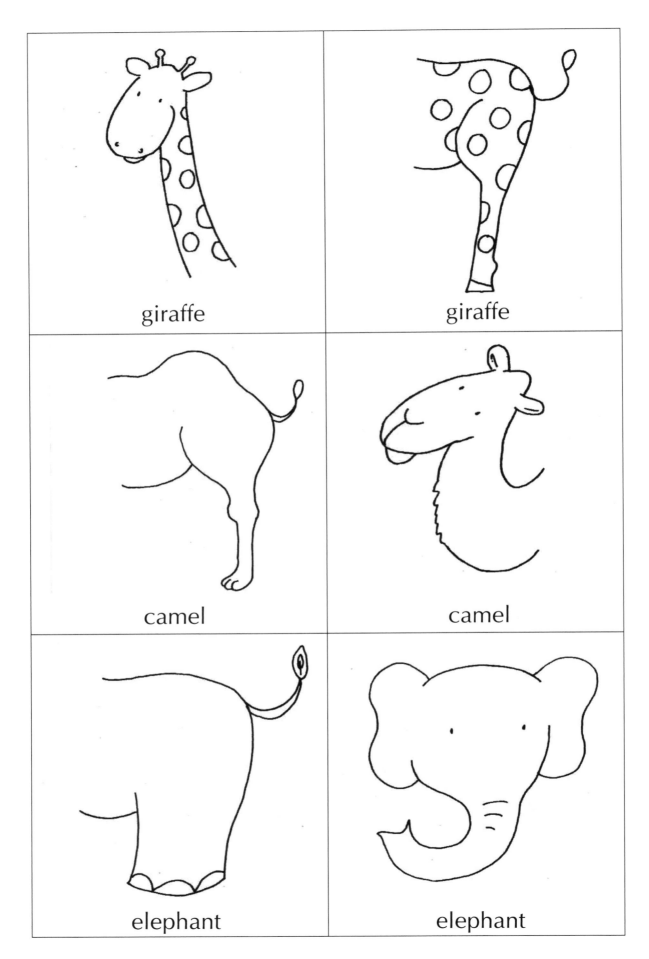

giraffe

giraffe

camel

camel

elephant

elephant

CHAPTER 4

Is that a butterfly?

by Claire Llewellyn (Macmillan Children's Books 2002)

The Very Hungry Caterpillar

by Eric Carle (Hamish Hamilton 1994)

Texts synopses

Through the conversations of Snail and Bee in *Is that a butterfly?*, the reader learns about the life cycle of a butterfly. The colourful illustrations and the surprise under the lift-up flap on every page make the never-ending story fascinating and enjoyable.

The Very Hungry Caterpillar is Eric Carle's enchanting, classic story about the life cycle of a butterfly. By following the caterpillar's development through the food it eats, the reader journeys along the different developmental stages in an amusing but unforgettable way, although this caterpillar is very much a fantasy!

Early learning goals from *Curriculum guidance for the foundation stage*, Communication, language and literacy:

- Show...how information can be found in non-fiction texts to answer questions about where, who, why and how.
- Extend their vocabulary, exploring the meanings and sounds of new words.

Objectives from the *National Literacy Strategy (YR)*:

- To use knowledge of familiar texts to re-enact or retell to others, recounting the main points in the correct sequence.
- To learn new words from their reading and shared experiences.

Objectives from the *National Literacy Strategy (Y1)*:

- To assemble information from own experience, e.g. food, pets; to use simple sentences to describe, based on examples from reading.
- To learn new words from reading and shared experiences, and to make collections of personal interest or significant words and words linked to particular topics.

Materials needed

- ■ *Is that a butterfly?* by Claire Llewellyn (Macmillan Children's Books 2002) and *The Very Hungry Caterpillar* by Eric Carle (Hamish Hamilton 1994)
- ■ Flip chart and marker pens (see 'Preparation'), pictures of butterflies (optional)
- ■ White paper, paint and paintbrushes, plastic headbands, card, templates of the butterfly's life cycle (see 'Preparation'), scissors, glue
- ■ Old, clean tights or stockings, pipe cleaners, cardboard cylinders, wax crayons and cheese grater (see 'Preparation'), iron, old but clean cotton cloth or tea towel without loop pile, usually used for drying glasses
- ■ Food and utensils for a food preparation and/or cooking session, as required

Optional materials for other activities

- ■ Butterfly hatching kit
- ■ Plants, flowers and shrubs that attract butterflies, outdoor garden area
- ■ Selection of books about butterflies
- ■ Butterfly matching cards (see 'Preparation')

Preparation

- ▲ On the first page of the flip chart draw four arrows in a circle with a break between each one and *The life cycle of a butterfly* written in the centre (see Figure 4.1 on p. 36).
- ▲ Use Photocopiable Sheet 9 (p. 40) to make templates of the butterfly's life cycle for the children in Group B.
- ▲ Prepare antennae and wings for Group C.
- ▲ Grate different coloured wax crayons using the coarsest section of the cheese grater.
- ▲ Make a set of butterfly matching cards using Photocopiable Sheets 10 and 11 (pp. 41 and 42).

Introducing the text

- Show the front cover of *Is that a butterfly?* to the children and ask them to join with you as you read the title. Spend a few moments talking about the illustration on the cover. What insects can the children see? What colours are on the butterfly's wings? How many legs does it have? Can anyone say why the butterfly is near the flower?
- Share the book with the children, tracking the text with your finger as you read. Pause from time to time to ask the children a relevant question. For example, when Snail says, 'Butterflies always lay their eggs under a leaf', before you read the rest, ask the children if they know why; or when Bee asks, 'What's so good about prickly spines?' ask the children if they know the answer. When you're looking at the illustrations, encourage the children to guess what might be under each flap before it is lifted. Invite different children to come out and lift the flaps.

- When you have finished reading the text, explore the book in more detail and involve the children in a recount of the main stages of the butterfly's life cycle. Ask the children some questions to jog their memories: *Can anyone remember the first thing that happens? What happens to the eggs? How long does it take for the eggs to hatch? What do the caterpillars do all day long? What happens when they become fat? After they have grown new skins, what do the caterpillars do? Can anyone remember the name of the hard case where the caterpillar hides itself? What's going on inside the chrysalis? What happens to the chrysalis in the end? How long does it take for the butterfly to develop and come out?* If the children need a bit of help to remember, look back at the appropriate part of the text and reread it together. As you talk about each stage of the butterfly's development, invite one of the children to come and draw a picture on the life-cycle diagram prepared on the flip chart. According to achievement level, invite some of the children to write a label, caption and/or sentence for each stage. Alternatively, invite the children to tell you what to write for each stage and scribe for them. If you have some pictures of butterflies, spend some time looking at them and discussing them in terms of shape, colour, size and so on.

- When you feel that the children are really confident about the life cycle of the butterfly, share *The Very Hungry Caterpillar*. As you read, track the text with your finger and invite the children to join in with you. Pause at relevant places and encourage the children to predict what might happen next. Because of the pattern of the story and the way the illustrations are presented, the children should be able to make plausible guesses. For example, if you read the 'Wednesday' page and then ask *What do you think will happen next?*, the children should be able to predict that the caterpillar will eat *four* (because of the counting-on number pattern in the story) *strawberries* (because one strawberry is visible for the next page) *on Thursday* (because of the days-of-the-week pattern in the story), *but still be hungry* (because he always is!). When you have finished reading, ask the children whether they enjoyed the book. Encourage them to tell you why or why not. Can they explain why there are holes in most of the pages? Do they think the caterpillar could really have eaten all these things? Can they say why or why not? Which is their favourite part of the book? Why? Which is their favourite food of those eaten by the caterpillar? Why? Name different days of the week (in sequence or out of order, as you think best for your group of children) and ask the children whether they can remember what the caterpillar ate on that day. Look at the page that shows the chrysalis. Can the children tell you what word Eric Carle uses for the chrysalis? (Cocoon.) Does anyone know what a cocoon is? Explain to the children that the two words mean the same thing – they are both words for the 'house' or outer protective covering for the caterpillar. Can anyone tell you the word for the caterpillar itself when it's inside the chrysalis? (Pupa.) Does anyone know of other insects that make a cocoon or chrysalis to develop in? For example, a silkworm. Before you finish, invite the children once more to give a recount of the four main stages of a real butterfly's life cycle.

Focus activities

Group A: Help the children to make antennae using the plastic headbands and card (see Figure 4.2 on p. 37), and to make large pairs of wings. Let the children pattern and colour the wings as they like and then encourage them to use their props in their imaginative play.

Group B: Let the children make their own charts showing the life cycle of the butterfly. They can cut out and colour as they like the templates of each stage of the life cycle, from Photocopiable Sheet 9. They should then stick the templates onto a sheet of card, following the cycle that was drawn on the flip chart during the introductory session. Encourage them to write labels, captions and/or sentence(s) about each stage of the life cycle.

Group C: Use the legs of old tights for making caterpillars. Cut the required length of leg (include the foot) and stuff its length to make the body of the caterpillar. You can give it the segmented appearance by winding a piece of thread around the width of the body every so often, gently tightening and then tying it. Push pipe cleaners through the base and bend them down to form the legs; push pipe cleaners through the head end for antennae. Mix green (or required colour) paint fairly thickly and paint the caterpillar's body. Make eyes from white card and glue them on when the paint has dried. Encourage the children to write labels, captions and/or sentence(s) about their caterpillar models.

Group D: Help the children make 3D butterflies. Use the cardboard cylinders for the body, with eyes painted at one end. Draw symmetrical outlines of the wings on large sheets of white paper and cut them out. Scatter the grated wax crayons onto one wing and fold the other one over. Put the clean glass cloth or tea towel on top and gently press it with a warm iron – don't be tempted to move the iron about. (If this part is done with the children around, you will need to have another adult with you to supervise them. Make sure the iron and the children are kept well away from each other!) The wax melts with the heat of the iron and the colours mix, making interesting patterns. Let the wax dry before fastening the wings to the body. Hang the butterflies from the ceiling. Encourage the children to write labels, captions and/or sentence(s) about their butterflies.

Group E: Have some fun cooking/food sessions exploring some of the food eaten by the very hungry caterpillar. For example, make a chocolate cake (see *Literacy Play for the Early Years* Book 1: *Learning through fiction* (p. 64) for a recipe), some cupcakes or a cherry pie (see Figures 4.3 and 4.4 for recipes); or have a cheese and/or salami tasting session. (Use the opportunity to read the text on the packets of ingredients together with the children.) Make sure none of the children is allergic to any of the foods and remind them to wash their hands before they begin.

Other structured play activities

- Invest in a hatching kit and share the thrill of following the development of real caterpillars into butterflies. You can get hold of kits from: www.greengardener.co.uk or www.small-life.co.uk
- Turn your outside area into a butterfly garden by planting some 'butterfly friendly' plants and shrubs. You can get more information, help and advice from: www.butterflies.com or www.butterflywebsite.com. Alternatively, visit your local garden centre and ask advice about which plants will thrive in your setting's environment.
- Make large butterflies for a display. Cut out the main shape, paint one wing and fold the other over, carefully pressing the two halves together to give symmetrical patterns.
- Give the butterfly matching cards to play snap, pelmanism or matching games. Encourage the children to look very carefully at the patterns on the wings in order to match the pairs of butterflies.
- Visit a butterfly house. By typing *Butterfly Gardens* into the search engine of your computer, you will find which places there are to visit near you.
- Leave out a selection of books about butterflies and caterpillars plus, if possible, a story

sack for imaginative play. Some suitable titles are *Ben Plants a Butterfly Garden* by Petty Kate (Macmillan Children's Books 2001), *The Caterpillar that Roared* by Michael Lawrence (Dorling Kindersley 2000), *Elmer and the Butterfly* by David McKee (Andersen Press 2002), *From Caterpillar to Butterfly* by Deborah Heiligman (HarperCollins 1996), *Are you a butterfly?* by Judy Allen and Tudor Humphries (Kingfisher 2002) and *Minibeast Pets – Caterpillars* (Hodder Wayland 1999).

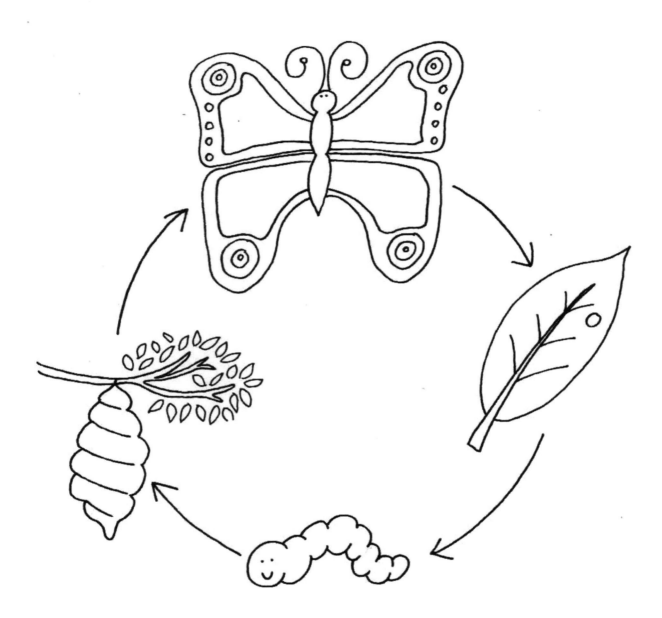

Figure 4.1 A diagram of the butterfly's life cycle

Step 1

Fold paper in half and draw the required outline plus 'bridge'. Cut out, making sure fold is not cut.

Step 2

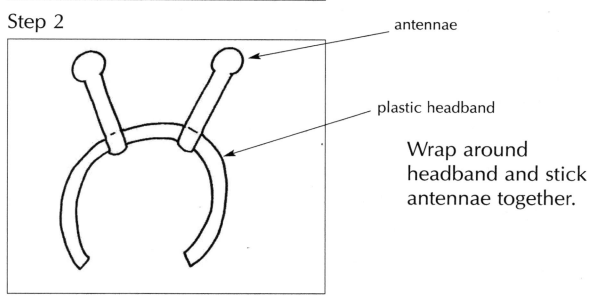

antennae

plastic headband

Wrap around headband and stick antennae together.

Step 3

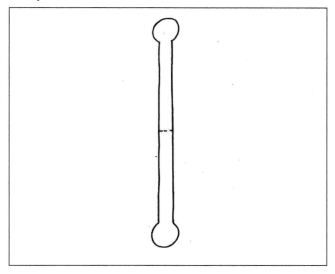

You could also make a pair of wings out of card, and tie them to the child with string.

Figure 4.2 How to make antennae for role-play

Cupcakes (microwave recipe, makes 12 small cakes)

Ingredients

50 g butter or margarine
50 g caster sugar
125 g self-raising flour
Paper bun cases

1 large egg
3 tablespoons milk
a few drops of vanilla, lemon or
orange essence, according to taste

Method

Cream the sugar and butter together until light and fluffy. Beat together the egg and the milk with the vanilla/lemon/orange essence. Add the egg mixture and flour (sieved in) alternately to the creamed sugar and butter mixture, beating well between each addition. Put the mixture into 12 paper bun cases and cook them six at a time in the microwave oven. Arrange the six bun cases in a circle on a flat plate and microwave on a High power setting for 2 minutes. Let them cool on a wire tray before decorating them as you like. You could make glacé icing (see below) to put on the top of cakes, decorated with cherries, 'hundreds and thousands' sugar strands or grated chocolate.

Glacé icing

Ingredients
125 g icing sugar
1–2 tablespoons warm water
Colouring or flavouring if required

Method

Sieve the sugar into a bowl and gently add the water, and flavouring or colouring if required, stirring well until it becomes a smooth consistency. It should coat the back of a spoon thickly, without running off. Spread the icing on the top of the cake(s) and sprinkle with your chosen topping – you need to do this fairly quickly as the icing hardens.

Figure 4.3 How to make cupcakes

Cherry Pie (with shortcrust pastry)

Ingredients

50 g margarine

50 g caster sugar

250 g plain flour

Cold water

50 g lard

½ teaspoon salt

2 tins cherry pie filling

Method

Preheat the oven to 200°C or Gas Mark 6. Sieve together the flour and salt. Cut the fats into small pieces and rub them into the flour until the mixture looks like fine breadcrumbs. Slowly add enough water, mixing with a knife to form a stiff dough. Put the dough onto a lightly floured surface and knead it gently until it is smooth. Cut it into two pieces, one slightly larger than the other. Roll out the larger piece and line the bottom of a pie dish with it. Put the cherry pie filling into the dish. Roll out the smaller piece of dough and cover the top of the dish with it, sealing the edges together with a little water. Prick holes in the top. Bake for 20–25 minutes or until the pastry is golden brown. Cool on a wire tray.

Note: MAKE SURE THE PIE IS COMPLETELY COLD BEFORE ALLOWING THE CHILDREN TO TASTE IT. THE CHERRY FILLING BECOMES EXTREMELY HOT DURING COOKING.

Figure 4.4 How to make cherry pie

The life cycle of a butterfly

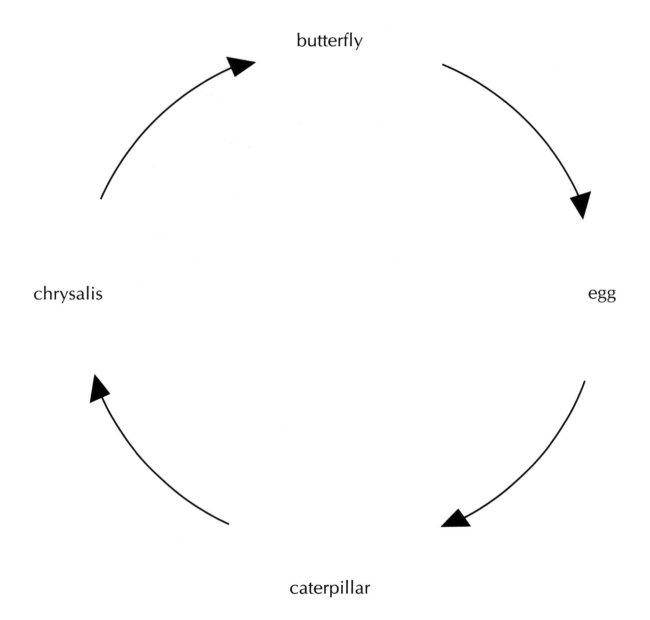

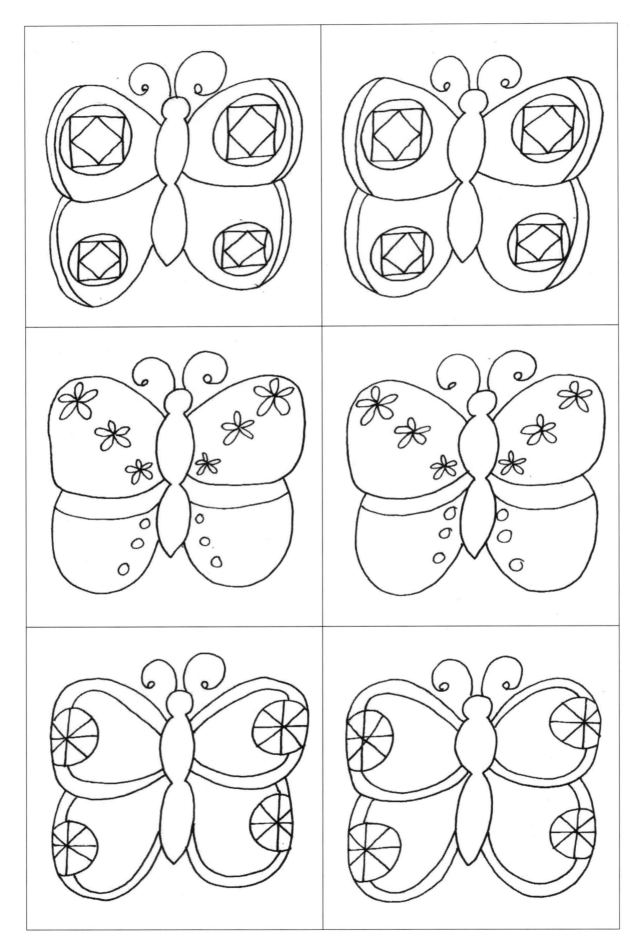

CHAPTER 5

What's under the bed?

by Mick Manning and Brita Granström (Franklin Watts 1996)

Text synopsis

The book follows the underground adventures of two children who start off by looking under the bed and end up going on a journey that takes them right to the earth's core.

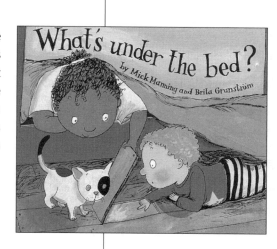

Early learning goals from *Curriculum guidance for the foundation stage,* Communication, language and literacy:

- Sustain attentive listening, responding to what they have heard by relevant comments, questions or actions.
- Show...how information can be found in non-fiction texts to answer questions about where, who, why and how.

Objectives from the *National Literacy Strategy (YR)*:

- To reread a text to provide context cues to help read unfamiliar words.
- To use knowledge of familiar texts to re-enact or retell to others, recounting the main parts in the correct sequence.

Objectives from the *National Literacy Strategy (Y1)*:

- To predict what a given book might be about from a brief look at both front and back covers, including blurb, title, illustration; to discuss what it might tell in advance of reading and check to see if it does.
- To write labels for drawings and diagrams.
- To produce extended captions, e.g. to explain paintings in wall displays or to describe artefacts.

Materials needed

- ■ *What's under the bed?* by Mick Manning and Brita Granström (Franklin Watts 1996), flip chart and marker pens, layer sequence cards (see 'Preparation'), card, scissors, glue, Blu-tack
- ■ Magnifying glasses, perspex or clear plastic tank, different coloured, size and textured materials for model of strata (see 'Preparation') such as play sand, lentils, pebbles, polystyrene packing chips, etc.
- ■ Clear plastic empty water/juice bottles, blotting paper, broad bean seeds, absorbent paper or paper kitchen-towels, water
- ■ Clay or other malleable materials (e.g. plasticine, play dough, wax, etc.), kiln (optional), paints and paintbrushes, materials to make a cave (e.g. brown paper, card, paints, etc.)

Optional materials for other activities

- ■ Dressing-up clothes, play tunnel and large construction blocks for imaginative play
- ■ Layer sequence cards (see 'Preparation'), card, scissors, glue, Blu-tack
- ■ A selection of books about the earth, caves and cave paintings, crystals and gems, volcanoes, dinosaurs, etc.

Preparation

- ▲ Using Photocopiable Sheets 12 and 13 (pp. 47 and 48) make some layer sequence cards.

Introducing the text

You may choose to introduce the text over several sessions:

- Spend a few minutes looking at the covers of the book and discussing with the children what they think is under the bed. Have any of the children ever been there when floorboards in their house were lifted? Ask them to share with the others what they saw underneath. Before you start to read, ask the children to guess what the book might be about. Jot a few key words from their suggestions on the flip chart and tell the children they can look at their ideas again at the end and see whether they guessed correctly.

- Share the book with the children, pausing at appropriate places to let the children answer the questions posed in the text (*What's under the . . . ?*), or to predict what might come next, or to explore the illustrations. As you go through the book, make sure you read all of the main text (in the larger typeface) on each page before you read the smaller print – often ideas from the main text are explored in the small print, and wouldn't make sense to the children if they haven't explored the main points first. While you are reading the text, encourage the children to join in as they see the pattern emerging and can remember the order of subterranean levels. When you have finished reading, ask the children whether they enjoyed the book. Can they tell you why or why not? Did they find it interesting? Which parts did they like best? Why? Was there anything in the book they didn't like very much? Why not? Look at their predictions about the book's content written on the flip chart at the beginning of the session. Did anyone guess correctly?

- Explore the book in more detail. Read it again, encouraging the children to join in with you, and exploring the illustrations as you go along. Ask relevant questions to stimulate discussion. For example, talk about the mites and bedbugs on the first page and ask whether anyone is allergic to mites – do their beds have to vacuumed at home? Has anyone ever had a mouse's nest in their house? Ask them to tell everyone about it. Look at any pipes there may be in the setting, such as those leading to and from the radiators and sinks. Explain that these are carried on under the floor and through the walls where we can't see, but the places look similar to the picture in the book. Does anyone know what *insulate* means? Do any of the children have insulated pipes at home? Ask them to tell you about how their pipes are insulated. Can anyone tell you why the pipes have to be kept warm? Has anyone ever had a burst pipe in their house? What happened? Talk about how plants and trees support themselves by growing roots in the soil level; discuss the insects and minibeasts that can be found in the soil. Have the children ever seen an ants' nest? Do they know what *colony* means? Can anyone tell you where we might go on a train in a tunnel? Have any of the children travelled this way? Does anyone know the correct word for the long moving staircase that the book talks about? Where else might we see escalators? Have the children ever seen dinosaurs' bones like those in the book? Where? Ask them to tell you about it. Can anyone tell you what a fossil is? Talk about the stalagmites and stalactites in the cave. Has anyone been in a cave and seen stalagmites and stalactites? Ask the children what coal is or, if they don't know, ask what we do with it. Explain that nowadays we don't have many coal mines left in the UK. Spend a bit of time looking at the crystals and precious metals in the next layer. Where might the children see these? Explain that our precious rings and jewellery are made from these minerals. Have the children seen pictures of a volcano on the television? Explain that a volcano is caused by melted rock called magma that has burst up from the inner parts of the earth. Talk about the very centre of the earth and that is it hotter than anyone can ever imagine. This is called the *earth's core* – can anyone suggest why?

- Give out the layer sequence cards, one per child, and play a game where the children holding the cards have to come out and stand in a line, in the correct order of the earth's layers, starting from the floorboards. Challenge the children to find the right sequence without receiving any clues from you. According to achievement level, they could play the game in reverse, following the return journey of the children in *What's under the bed?*

Focus activities

Group A: Take the children outside with the magnifying glasses and explore the soil for minibeasts. Encourage the children to look for things on the surface of the soil first. Which creatures like to live on top of the soil, in the light and dry environment? Then let the children dig a hole and see what they can find under the surface. Lift a few stones and encourage them to examine what lives in the place underneath. Which creatures like to live in the damp and dark places? When you go back inside, ask the children to draw the creatures they found, and write labels, captions and/or sentence(s) about their discoveries. (Note: Make sure the children wash their hands and scrub their nails when they come back inside. Handling soil can be a very messy and unhygienic activity!)

Group B: Help the children to make a model of the layers of the earth following the sequence in *What's under the bed?* Use the perspex tank and line it with the different coloured, size and textured materials to show each stratum. Remind the children that they'll have to put the earth's core on the bottom of the tank. Make a model house for the top; use a twig as a model tree. Place an object in each layer, to represent what can be found in it. For example, use coloured beads to represent the precious crystals, a small plastic container on its side to represent the secret cave and plastic bones to represent the dinosaurs. The children should write labels, captions and/or sentence(s) to explain their model.

Group C: To show the children how plants have roots, grow some broad beans. Soak the broad bean seeds overnight in water. Cut the bottoms off the plastic water/juice bottles, to a height of about 15 cm (don't use glass jars for safety reasons), line them with the blotting paper and fill the centre hole with the absorbent paper or paper kitchen-towels. Place the broad bean seeds between the blotting paper and the jar so that the children can see them easily. Pour in enough water to make sure the blotting paper and the centre paper are wet – keep the containers well watered. Put them in a warm place out of direct sunlight and don't allow them to dry out. The children will begin to see some results in a few days. Help the children to label and write captions for their beans, particularly the roots. Depending on the time of year, you could plant the beans in some pots filled with soil, or outside in the garden, and encourage the children to look after them and crop the vegetables when they're ready.

Group D: Give the children the clay or alternative malleable materials and ask them to make something that they can use such as a vase, a plate, a cup or a saucer. Let them decorate their objects when the clay has been fired or the other malleable materials are dry and ready for painting. The children should write labels, captions and/or sentence(s) about their clay objects.

Group E: Let the children turn the Home Corner into a cave. Line the walls of the cave with brown paper; make some stalagmites and stalactites using sugar paper folded into cones and painted brown. Encourage the children to look at pictures of prehistoric cave paintings and then let them make some paintings of their own to decorate the walls of their cave. Let the children spend time in imaginative play in their cave.

Other structured play activities

- Have some minibeast colonies in the setting and let the children see the insects' life cycles at first hand. Visit www.small-life.co.uk for a comprehensive list of school projects and advice about appropriate insects or minibeasts for classrooms, and how to keep them.
- Let the children use the play tunnel and large construction blocks to make the route taken by the children in *What's under the bed?* on their journey. They could draw pictures of bones and dinosaurs, crystals and coal and stick them on the different levels of the earth. Let them dress up and role-play the journey. When they get to the magma layer, let them wear a spacesuit as protective clothing. If the setting doesn't have spacesuits, let the children make helmets and gloves for their role-play.
- Give the children the layer sequence cards, Blu-tack and a sheet of card large enough to make a chart. Ask them to put the cards in sequence and use the Blu-tack to stick them onto the sheet of card to make a chart showing the layers of the earth. They should put the cards in a vertical rather than horizontal line. Let them refer to *What's under the bed?* to jog their memories if they need a bit of support. Ask them to write labels, captions and/or sentence(s) to explain each level of their chart.
- Arrange a trip through a tunnel, if possible on a train, as shown in the book. Arrange a visit to an exhibition of dinosaurs' bones and skeletons. Afterwards, let the children make up role-plays and write and draw about their trips.
- Have a selection of books about the earth, caves and cave paintings, crystals and gems, volcanoes, dinosaurs and so on. Leave them in the Book Corner for the children to explore at their own leisure.

floorboards

wires and pipes

soil and plant roots

ants

clay

tunnel

dinosaur

secret cave

coal mine

crystals and gold

magma

the earth's core

CHAPTER 6

How Do Your Senses Work?

by Judy Tatchell (Usborne Publishing 1997)

Text synopsis

With cartoon-type illustrations and an easy-to-follow text, the book introduces each of the five senses that humans have and it also explores the more efficient senses that some animals have. Using simple, yet clear language, the information is put across in an appeal-

ing way and also helps the children to extend their vocabulary as it introduces the correct terminology.

Early learning goals from *Curriculum guidance for the foundation stage*, Communication, language and literacy:

- Write their own names and other things such as labels and captions and begin to form simple sentences, sometimes using punctuation.
- Extend their vocabulary, exploring the meanings and sounds of new words.

Objectives from the *National Literacy Strategy (YR)*:

- To learn new words from their reading and shared experiences.
- To write labels or captions for pictures or drawings.
- To write sentences to match pictures or sequences of pictures.

Objectives from the *National Literacy Strategy (Y1)*:

- To learn new words from reading and shared experiences, and to make collections of personal interest or significant words and words linked to particular topics.
- To write captions for their own work, e.g. for display, in class books.

Materials needed

- *How Do Your Senses Work?* by Judy Tatchell (Usborne Publishing 1997), flip chart and marker pens, radio
- Materials to make a spinner (see 'Preparation'), card, glue, scissors (or if possible, pinking shears), string
- A selection of objects with different textures (e.g. a piece of velvet, a wooden numeral, a walnut, a cotton wool ball, a key, a square of jelly) making sure there are more objects than children in the group, a feely bag, describing word cards (optional – see 'Preparation')
- Materials to make flower templates (see 'Preparation'), crayons or coloured marker pens, cotton wool balls, straws, play dough, a selection of different scents such as lemon, perfume, coffee, strawberry, curry and so on
- A selection of different foods for each area of the tongue (see 'Preparation'), giant tongues (see 'Preparation')
- Cassette recorder/player and blank cassette; paper, pencils and coloured marker pens

Optional materials for other activities

- A selection of different foods for each area of the tongue and a set of labelled trays, each with a taste word written on it (i.e. *sweet, salty, bitter* and *sour*)
- Binoculars, telescope, magnifying glasses and microscope, a selection of items to look at through the magnifying glasses and microscope
- Camera and film, cassette player/recorder, a selection of recorded tapes featuring stories and poems, the books that accompany the stories and poems, blank cassettes

Preparation

- ▲ Use Photocopiable Sheet 14 (p. 55) to make templates of spinners for Group A.
- ▲ Make a set of describing word cards, each with a 'feely' word such as *soft, lumpy, sticky, hard, cold, stretchy* and so on.
- ▲ Use Photocopiable Sheet 15 (p. 56) to make templates of flowers for Group C.
- ▲ Collect a variety of foods that stimulate the different taste bud regions in the tongue. For example, *sour*: lemon, sour cream; *salty*: crisps, bacon; *sweet*: biscuits, sweets; *bitter*: coffee, black chocolate. Have small portions for each child to taste. (Note: Make sure none of the children is allergic to any of the foods or that they do not have any special dietary requirements.)
- ▲ Make a giant tongue for each child in Group D with the different taste areas labelled on it (see Figure 6.1 on p. 54).

Introducing the text

- Look at the cover of the book with the children and spend a few moments discussing what it might be about. Ask them what *senses* means – if they're not sure, can they work it out from the 'blurb', the speech bubbles and the little fantasy figures in the cover's illustrations? Read the first section (*What are senses?*) inviting the children to read some of the text and/or the speech bubbles. Before you open the flap, discuss with the children what it would be like if we couldn't see, hear, touch, smell or taste. Do they think it would be enjoyable? Why not? If any of the children uses an aid such as glasses or a hearing aid, take the opportunity to invite them to explain to the others how the aid works – be sensitive to the children's feelings, however, and don't force them to do this if they prefer not to. Tell the children that aids like these help a person's sense, such as seeing or hearing, to work more efficiently.

- Share the rest of book with the children taking time to explore each section. Encourage the children to do any of the little activities mentioned in the book. For example, using the radio for the hearing activity on page 7. When you have finished reading, ask the children whether they enjoyed the book. Encourage them to tell you why or why not. Was there a part they particularly liked? Why? Was there a part they didn't like very much? Why not? Ask them again what *senses* means – can they name the five senses?

- Explore the text in more detail. Are there any words that the children aren't sure about? For example, *nerves, murky, receptors* and *mucus*. Because each section of the book explains the meanings of these words in both pictures and text, take time to discuss them thoroughly and make sure the children grasp the meanings. Invite different children to come out and role-play the cartoon sketches from each section. For example, when the boy steals the girl's bike, when the girl smells fire or when the boy decides it's time to change his socks. Encourage the children to use the correct vocabulary in their role-play. As you look at each section in more detail, encourage the children to expand on the information given. For example, can they add to the list of hot, cold, soft, hard, tickly and scratchy things that we can feel? Can they name other sour, salty, bitter and sweet foods that we can taste? In the final section, which talks about animals with senses that are more developed and efficient than our own, can the children come up with other examples? For instance, birds of prey that can see a potential meal from a very high position, or snakes that can smell with their tongues.

- Let the children take time to examine the illustrations in detail. Invite them to explain to you the think bubbles for the children in the introductory section. For example, why does the little boy look at the dog and think *I think I'll stay away!!*? Why does the girl eating the lemon think *Ughh! Spit it out!!*? Ask the children whether they think that nerves really do have little creatures marching up to the brain carrying messages on posters. Spend a few moments comparing the picture of what it's like to see in the dark and what difference a light makes. How is each colour different? For example, yellow becomes white in the dark and red turns grey. Tell the children that dogs don't see colours as brightly as we do because the receptors in their eyes are mostly made up of rods and far fewer cones. Are there any illustrations in the book that the children find funny? For example, the cartoon of the boy listening to his personal stereo and not being able to hear his Mum saying, *Tidy your room now!!* Or the boy with cheesy socks. Can anyone explain the picture of the tongue and why it has different colours in the picture? Let them look at each other's tongues (if they haven't already done so) to see the bumps containing their taste buds. Invite two volunteers to come out and show the others where their different tasting areas are – let one child use a clean lollipop stick or straw to gently point to each taste area on the other child's tongue. Does anyone have an experience about their senses that they'd like to tell the others about?

Focus activities

Group A: Let the children make a spinner using the template on Photocopiable Sheet 14. If they cut out the circle with pinking shears, their spinners will have a more interesting edge. (Make sure that all children are careful when cutting out their templates.) They should thread string through the two holes and then tie the ends. Show them how to 'wind up' the thread (see the instructions on the photocopiable sheet) and then spin the circle. Ask them what happens to the colours – what do they see? They should tell you and/or write down what they noticed, according to achievement level.

Group B: Let the children play a game with the objects in the feely bag. They should take turns to take hold of something in the bag, feel it and describe it – you may have to suggest some describing words to get them going. When they have described what the object feels like, they should guess what it is, then remove it from the bag. If their guess is right, they 'keep' the object and pass the bag to the next child. An alternative version is to spread the describing word cards out on the table and the child who is feeling the object in the bag should place it next to a card that describes it. Are there some objects that could go beside more than one description card?

Group C: Let the children make fragrant flowers by colouring the flower template (Photocopiable Sheet 15) and sticking cotton wool balls in the baking cases, adding a different fragrance to each ball of cotton wool. Stick the baking case to the centre of the flower. Attach the flower to a straw and then secure the flower on its 'stem' in a ball of play dough. Let the children savour the aromas in their own time. According to achievement level, the children could write labels, captions and/or sentence(s) about the scents in their flowers. Challenge the children to make up names for their aromatic blooms! *

Group D: Give the different foods and the giant tongues (see Figure 6.1) to the children. Let them taste each item of food and decide which area of tongue to put it on. They could work in pairs or as a group for support. Encourage them to make labels, captions and/or sentence(s) about their experiment. Ask them to make a table display of their experiments. If the display is to stay there for a while, the children could draw the foods on the appropriate parts of the tongues. Alternatively, you could make sure that fresh supplies of the food are available to enable the other children in the setting to have a go at the experiments themselves. In this case, leave out a supply of tongue templates as well.

Group E: Take the children, cassette recorder and blank cassette outside and help the children to record some of the noises they can hear. Encourage them to listen carefully, differentiate between the various sounds and then choose which ones they want to record. When you go back inside, ask them to listen to their recording and identify the different sounds. They should draw pictures of the things that made the sounds and write labels, captions and/or sentence(s) to go with their drawings.

Other structured play activities

- Have a selection of different fruits and vegetables, washed, sliced and ready to taste. Play a game where the children are blindfolded and have to taste the fruits and vegetables before guessing what they are. If they don't know the names of any of the fruits or vegetables, encourage them to describe how they taste, such as bitter, sour, salty or sweet and so on.

---

* My thanks to Kevin Kelman and Alice Sharpe for this idea ('Activities to appreciate smell', *Nursery World*, 4 July 2002, pp. 12–13).

- Have a selection of different foods that can be classified into one of the categories of taste (sweet, salty, bitter and sour). Leave out the four trays with labels on them and let the children experiment with the foods, deciding which tray they should be put onto.
- Leave out the binoculars, telescope, magnifying glasses and microscope for the children to explore and play with in their own time. Let them use the microscope to examine the small items you have chosen.
- Load the film into the camera. Take the children outdoors and let each of them take a photograph. Encourage them to look carefully before deciding what they want to take a picture of. Have the film developed as soon as possible so that the children have feedback about their work fairly quickly. Let them make a book of their photographs, with captions and labels about their pictures.
- Leave out the cassette player and a selection of taped stories and poems for the children to listen to at leisure. Leave the accompanying books out as well so the children can follow the text. Encourage them to tape their own stories and poems onto a blank cassette for other children to listen to.
- Let the children collect objects from around the setting, both indoors and outside, that have different textures. Encourage them to feel with the tips of their fingers in order to choose appropriate objects. Make a 'feely' display of their collections and encourage them to write labels or captions to go with each object. Some things the children might collect are velvet and fake fur, rough pebbles, sandpaper, glue, sticks, dry leaves, spiky twigs, bubble wrap and so on.
- Take the children outside and spend some time talking about what you can smell. For example, car fumes, tumble-drying perfume, food cooking, bonfire smoke, post-rain soil, flowers and so on. Do the same thing indoors – how are the smells different? Which do the children prefer? Let them draw or paint pictures of the things they smelt. Encourage them to write labels, captions and/or sentence(s) about their pictures.

This bit tastes
bitter things

This bit tastes
sour things

This bit tastes
sour things

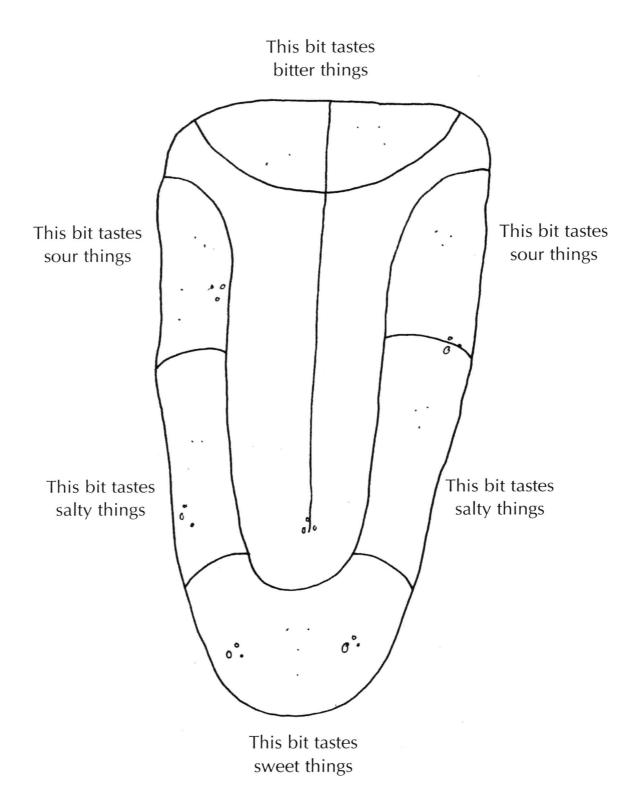

This bit tastes
salty things

This bit tastes
salty things

This bit tastes
sweet things

Figure 6.1 Use this to make a template of a giant-sized tongue

Make a colour spinner. Colour the sections and then thread string through the holes. Knot the ends and have fun twirling your spinner.

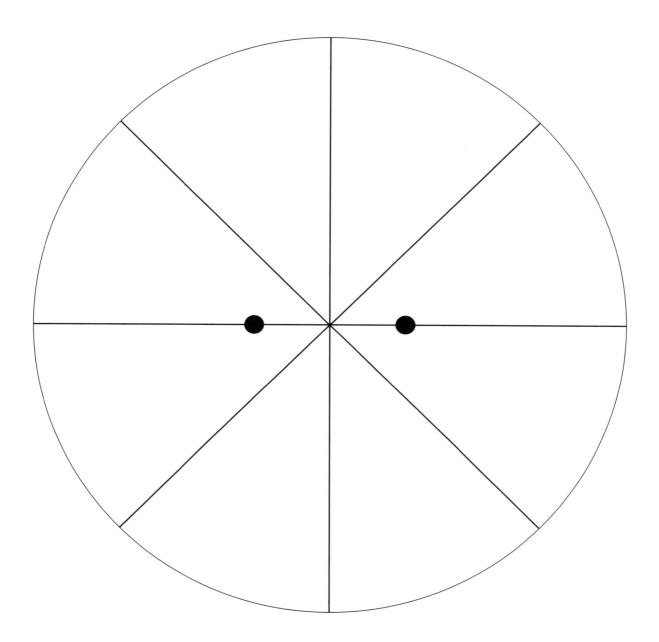

Flower template

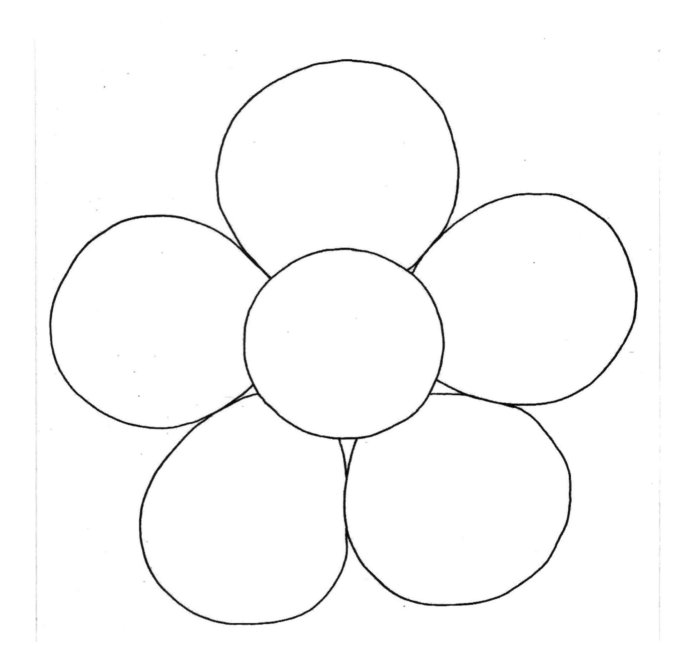

CHAPTER 7

Homes and Houses Then and Now

by Alastair Smith (Usborne Publishing 1999)

Text synopsis

The book has cartoon-type illustrations and information about the development of homes and housing in 'child-friendly' sections. It explores different types of housing, from people living in caves, to the different types of home that the children are familiar with today. The book also looks at homes in other countries such as Norway and Egypt. You can pitch the discussion to suit the achievement level of your children, going into as much or as little detail as you think appropriate.

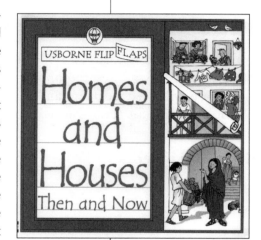

Early learning goals from *Curriculum guidance for the foundation stage*, Communication, language and literacy:

- Use language to imagine and recreate roles and experiences.
- Write...things such as labels and captions and begin to form simple sentences, sometimes using punctuation.

Objectives from the *National Literacy Strategy (YR)*:

- To recognise printed and handwritten words in a variety of settings.
- To understand that writing can be used for a range of purposes...

Objectives from the *National Literacy Strategy (Y1)*:

- To read and use captions, e.g. labels around the school, on equipment.
- To write captions for their own work, e.g. for display, in class books.

Because very young children find the concept of time difficult, you may have to put some of the historical information in the general context of 'long ago'. Try to relate the information you share with the children to similar experiences within their own lives. When discussing different aspects of homes and housing, encourage them to think of the same aspects in their own homes. So, for example when you are looking at heating systems in houses, the children can talk about the radiators, gas fires or storage heaters in their homes compared with the open fire in the middle of the floor in a Viking house.

Materials needed

- *Homes and Houses Then and Now* by Alastair Smith (Usborne Publishing 1999), a collection of pictures of the types of housing to be found in the area around the setting (see 'Preparation'), flip chart and marker pens (see 'Preparation')
- Paper, pencils, pens, coloured marker pens, a shoebox for each child in Group B, small play furniture or materials to make models of furniture as preferred, glue, paint, scissors
- House and people matching cards (see 'Preparation'), materials to make the street where your setting is (if you prefer to photograph the buildings instead of the children making them, you will need a camera and film)
- Furnish the house cards (see 'Preparation'), ground plan cards (see 'Preparation')

Optional materials for other activities

- Historical furniture and house cards

Preparation

- ▲ Get hold of some pictures showing the housing that is typical of your setting's environment and that the children will be able to identify with. For example, if your setting is in an inner-city area, you could have pictures of blocks of flats, terraced houses and a temple; if you are in a rural area, you're more likely to have stone cottages, farmhouses and village halls. Your local estate agent may be willing to let you have old photographs that are no longer needed and that reflect the type of housing to be found in your area.
- ▲ On the first page of the flip chart, draw a ground plan of a typical modern kitchen (see Figure 7.1 on p. 62). On the second page, draw a ground plan of a bungalow with four rooms, the kitchen (the same layout as the plan you drew on the first page), the bathroom, the bedroom and the living room. (Note: If the living room is known by another name in your locality, for example lounge or front room, use the word that is familiar to the children.) Put in the furniture, equipment, appliances and so on, and label them. Cover the plans over.
- ▲ Make a set of house and people matching cards using Photocopiable Sheets 16 and 17 (pp. 64 and 65).
- ▲ Make a set of furnish the house cards for each child in Group E using Photocopiable Sheets 18 and 19 (pp. 66 and 67). Make a ground plan for each child by dividing a sheet of card (minimum size A3) into four and label the 'rooms' *kitchen, bathroom, bedroom* and *living room* (or appropriate local word).

Introducing the text

You may choose to introduce the text over several sessions:

- Look at the cover with the children and spend a few moments discussing what the book might be about. Point out how the bottom part of the illustration shows some flats in ancient Rome and the top part shows modern flats. Spend a few moments comparing the clothes of the two sets of people. Together, read the 'blurb' on the back cover. Do they know what *apartment* means? What other word can we use? (Flat.) Can anyone tell you what a *medieval castle* is? Have any of the children visited a castle? Invite them to share their experiences. Read the first section of the book (*Long ago*) inviting the children to read some of the text. Are there any words that the children aren't sure about? For example, *gloomy, animal fat* or *frames* (for pictures). Help them to use the context and illustrations to work out the meanings of any new words. Before you open the flap, spend some time with the children talking about the outside of the cave dwelling: What is the door made from? Why aren't there any windows? How are the men dressed? Why? What are they carrying home? What for? Invite one of the children to open the flap and spend some time discussing the inside of the cave. How are the people keeping warm? How will they cook their meals? How will they eat their food? Are they going to eat just the meat from the deer? How do we know? Do the people have beds? Are they like ours? What's the difference? How is the cave lit? How is it decorated? Look at the small pictures on the opposite page that show the contrast between the facilities we enjoy today and the way the cave dwellers lived. Share the rest of the book with the children taking time to explore each section. Encourage them to predict what they'll discover underneath the flap on each page, and then invite different children to lift the flaps. Were their guesses correct? When you have finished reading, ask the children whether they enjoyed the book. Encourage them to tell you why or why not.
- Explore the text in more detail. Are there any words that the children aren't sure about? For example, *air conditioning, dingy, drifted, enemies* and *oxen*. Take time to discuss any new words thoroughly and make sure the children grasp the meanings. Invite different children to come out and role-play the cartoon sketches from each section. For example, the Viking family cooking stew in their one-room house, the knights defending their castle, the American pioneers travelling with their wagon or the modern-day children going on holiday in their motor home. Ask the children to give you a recount of some of the information they read in the book. For example, who lived in which parts of a Roman apartment house? (The poor people at the top and the rich people in the middle, with the shops on the ground floor.) How do people in a very cold country keep their houses warm? Can the children tell you how we protect our homes today?
- Let the children take plenty of time to examine the illustrations in detail and help them to make comparisons between past and present. For example, look at the Romans having a wash on page 11, compared with the modern-day shower and bath times in the apartment block on the opposite page; or contrast the inside of the pioneers' wagon with the interior of the present-day camper van. Invite the children to show you the sections they liked best. Ask them to tell you why they chose those sections. Which section did they like the least? Why? Are there any illustrations in the book that the children find funny? For example, the toilet room on page 11, or the lady singing in the bath on page 13. Discuss with the children the ways that the illustrations show the contrasts between modern houses and facilities and the earlier versions of the same things. Spend time exploring the differences in detail, encouraging the children to look carefully and spot the changes that have taken place over the years.
- Look at the pictures of housing in your area and discuss them together. Which pictures look

like the houses that the children live in? Do any of them live in homes that are different from the houses in your pictures? If so, invite them to talk about their houses and what they are like – get them to describe the outside and the inside of their homes. Do they have the same facilities, such as a sink and a bath or shower, a cooker and a fridge? Is it just the actual building that's different? Do any of the children have relatives that live in another part of the country (or indeed in another country!) where the houses are different from those in your locality? Ask them to tell you what these other houses are like. What about the facilities in their relatives' house? Encourage the children to tell you about their homes. How do they keep their homes warm? How are their meals cooked? How do they store their food? What do they sleep on? Do they have a garden? Do they share the building and/or the garden with other families? Are they near shops? If they could choose to live in any of the homes in *Homes and Houses Then and Now* (past or present) which one would it be? Why? Which would they really dislike living in? Why?

- Uncover the ground plan of the kitchen that you drew on the flip chart and ask the children if they can tell you what it is. Spend some time explaining to them that it's a picture of a kitchen drawn as if they were on the ceiling looking down. Invite them to identify the different features in the kitchen. Is there anything in their kitchens at home that is not in your plan? For example, a dishwasher or a central heating boiler. Is there room to draw one? Invite them to come and draw it. Have a look at the plan of the bungalow and spend time exploring each room. Again, can the children suggest things that are not on the plan you drew?

Focus activities

Group A: Ask the children to draw a simple plan of the kitchen in their own house, showing the appliances in the correct positions (see Figure 7.1). Let them look at your plan on the flip chart to jog their memories if they need a bit of support. According to achievement level, they could draw plans of every room in the house and make them into a book called *My house*. They should label their diagrams. Make a display of the plans and encourage the children to write a caption to go with their picture. If they have made books, leave these out for the other children to look at in their own time.

Group B: Ask the children to make 3D models of their house using a box. They can furnish their houses either with small play toys, or with models they make themselves. They should write labels, captions and/or sentence(s) to go with their models.

Group C: Give the house and people matching cards to the children and ask them to pair the right people to the right homes. Let them look at the book if they need a bit of support.

Group D: Make a wall chart of the street where your setting is. Take the children out to look at the buildings first and then let them draw or paint them. Alternatively, they could take photographs and use these to make up the frieze.

Group E: Give the furnish the house cards and ground plans to the children and ask them to place each piece of furniture in the right room. They could do this activity in pairs.

Other structured play activities

- Take the children for a walk in the locality around the setting. Encourage them to look carefully at the different types of housing and homes that they see on their walk. Take time to stop and talk about the features of different homes. For example, a bungalow has no upstairs, a block of flats has lots of smaller homes inside the same building, a Victorian house has attics, maybe a cellar and railings around the garden, a modern house may have an open-plan garden with no fence at all, some houses have a window on either side of the front door while others have just one window at the side. When you get back to the setting, together draw a simple map of your route, showing the different types of homes you saw. Let the children draw these houses (see Figure 7.2).

- Some museums have a lending service for their local schools, whereby they select artefacts that are relevant to a theme or topic and allow the children to handle them, examine them closely and even sometimes to play with them. Check what your local museum has to offer regarding household articles.

- If there's a museum near your setting that has recreated homes from the past (for example, Beamish Museum in County Durham, York Castle Museum or the Black Country Museum in the West Midlands) take the children for a first-hand experience of old-fashioned housing.

- Ask a grandma and grandad (or even a great-grandparent) to come into the setting and talk to the children about what their home life was like when they were little. If possible, have some pictures or artefacts from that period to show the children as well – most grandparents or great-grandparents will (at the time of writing) have experienced childhood during the period 1920s to 1950s, an era of quite a few changes in itself!

- Make a set of cards similar to those on Photocopiable Sheets 18 and 19 but showing historical furniture and houses. Let the children play a matching game where they have to put the furniture in the appropriate rooms. A Victorian house is particularly good for this game because it had so many rooms.

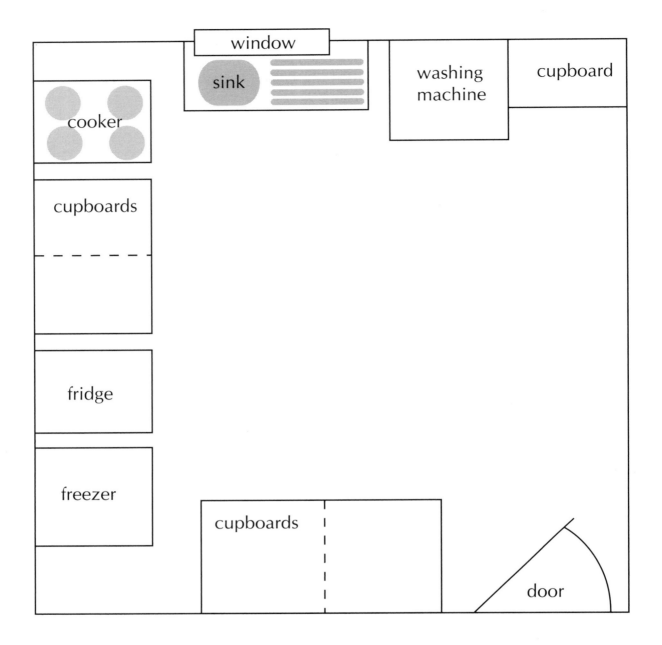

Figure 7.1 An example of the floor plan of a kitchen

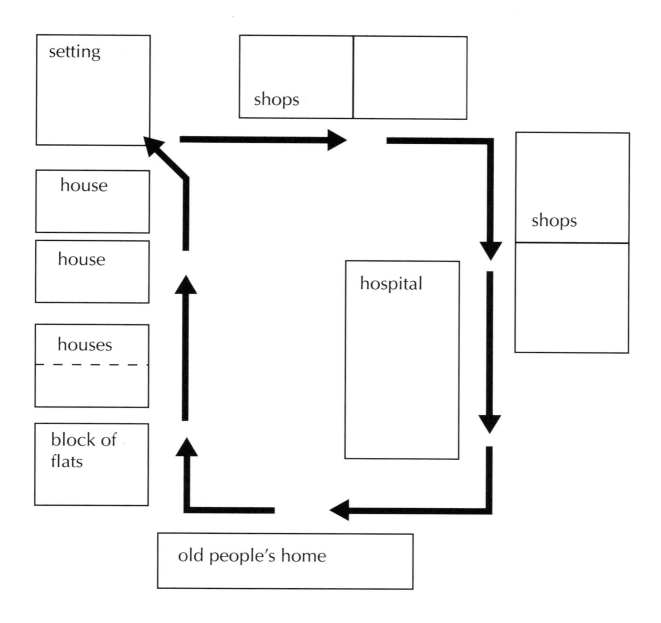

Figure 7.2 An example of a simple directional map of a walk

bath

handbasin

toilet

bed

wardrobe

chest of drawers

cooker

washing machine

sink

fridge

cupboards

sofa

armchairs

television

table and chairs

dresser

CHAPTER 8

Once There Were Giants

by Martin Waddell (Walker Books 1989)

My Family Tree Book

by Catherine Bruzzone (B Small Publishing 1996)

Texts synopses

Once There Were Giants is a story that follows the development of a baby, to whom Mum, Dad, Jill, John and Uncle Tom seem to be giants. As time passes, however, the giants shrink and eventually, the baby becomes a giant herself as her own baby looks up at her!

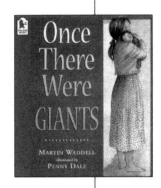

My Family Tree Book is an activity book that introduces the children to the concept of a family tree, by exploring from the child's immediate family to his or her extended family. It is filled with ideas at different stages and levels, which usefully help the children to see themselves in context.

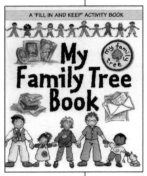

Early learning goals from *Curriculum guidance for the foundation stage*, Communication, language and literacy:

- Show...how information can be found in non-fiction texts to answer questions about where, who, why and how.
- Write their own names and other things such as labels and captions...

Objectives from the *National Literacy Strategy (YR)*:

- To reread frequently a variety of familiar texts, e.g. ...information books, captions, own and other children's writing.
- To think about and discuss what they intend to write, ahead of writing it.

Objectives from the *National Literacy Strategy (Y1)*:

- To write about events in personal experience linked to a variety of familiar incidents from stories.
- To write and draw simple instructions and labels for everyday classroom use, e.g. in role-play area for equipment.

Objectives from the *National Literacy Strategy (Y2)*:

- To use a variety of organisational devices... to indicate sequences and relationships.
- To use story structure to write about own experience in same/similar form.

Materials needed

- ■ *Once There Were Giants* by Martin Waddell (Walker Books 1989) and *My Family Tree Book* by Catherine Bruzzone (B Small Publishing 1996)
- ■ Photographs of the children's families (see 'Preparation'), flip chart and marker pens, Blu-tack
- ■ Paper, paints and paintbrushes, crayons or coloured marker pens, thick paper for zigzag books (see 'Preparation'), scissors, card, template of a family tree (see 'Preparation'), commercially produced pack of *Happy Families* cards, cassette recorder/player, blank cassette

Optional materials for other activities

- ■ Photographs of the children's families, card, baby photographs of the setting's staff, materials for making a frieze, *Happy Families* cards

Preparation

- ▲ Ask the children to bring in some photographs of themselves, their parents, brothers and sisters and, if possible, some of their grandparents and uncles and aunts. Make sure they have permission to bring the photos in. Ask each child in Group E for a funny story about something that happened when they were a baby – they may have to ask their parents for a bit of help with this one!
- ▲ On the first page of the flip chart, draw a simple family tree showing the relationships between the various family members in the book (see Figure 8.1 on p. 73). On the second page, draw a similar but blank family tree. Cover both pages.
- ▲ Make zigzag books by cutting a strip of thick paper long enough to make several 'pages', one for each member of the child's immediate family – six pages will allow for the child, two parents and three siblings. Fold the paper in concertina style, making sure the pages are equal in size.
- ▲ Using Photocopiable Sheet 20 (p. 75) make templates of a family tree.

Note: This project may raise issues of family and relationships, divorce and single-parenthood, adoption, etc. Be sensitive to the feelings of the children, particularly those who are personally affected. Use the opportunity to discuss positively and openly any general aspects of these issues that the children may ask about, without focusing on the situation of individual children.

Introducing the text

You may choose to introduce the text over several sessions and to do less or more than is explored here:

- Together look at the cover and title of *Once There Were Giants* and ask the children what they think the book might be about. Can they guess how giants and a tiny baby might be connected? Talk about the picture and 'blurb' on the back cover and ask the children what they think now. Do they think that adults would appear to be giants in a baby's eyes? Can they say why or why not?

- Share the text of the book, giving the children the opportunity to ask questions or predict what might come next as the commentary develops. When you have finished reading, ask the children whether they enjoyed the book. Can they say why or why not? Is the subject of the book familiar to them? If so, ask them to tell you how. Explore the text in more detail. Who is the narrator in the book? Can the children say when she is telling the story? How do they know? (If necessary, explain that it must be when she had grown up because at the end of the book, we can see the picture of her with her own baby and husband, and the other family members who are all much older.) Who are Jill and John in the book? Who is Uncle Tom? How is Uncle Tom related to Mum and Dad? Explain that he is the brother to either Mum or Dad. Can anyone tell you how the narrative changes from the early part of the book to the later parts? For example, early on in the book the baby says, 'There were Giants in our house', 'I sat at the table way up in the sky' and 'Dad was a dragon and he gave a roar' – are these things true? Why does the baby think they are? Whereas later the child/older girl/woman describes each situation factually. Can anyone suggest why this is? What do the children notice about the last couple of comments on each page? What do we want to do when we read the last two sentences on each page? Explain that this is a clever way of making us look at the pictures more closely.

- Look at the illustrations in more detail. What do the children notice about the body of the narrator as the book progresses? What about the other members of the family? Let the children compare the first and the last full-page illustrations – spend a bit of time discussing the differences. For example, there are six people in the first and eight in the last – who has joined the family? (Don and the new baby.) How and why do Mum, Dad, Uncle Tom, Jill and John all look very different? How has the room changed? How have the things for the baby changed? Are the toys different? Look at the changes in each picture through the book. Can the children tell you anything about the seasons and the weather in the illustrations? Can they suggest why the artist chose to do this? How do the clothes of the people change as time goes on? What about the kinds of toys and activities that we see in the pictures over the years? What are the changes in the way the narrator and her brother and sister play together and react to each other? What is the narrator's job when she's an adult? How do we know? Can the children identify each family member in the wedding picture? Who will tell the next episode of *Once There Were Giants*?

- Use the book as an introduction to the idea of a family tree. Uncover the family tree on the flip chart and talk about it with the children. Show them how the central figure is the narrator of the book, and how the relationships with the other members of the family are shown. Help the children to see in terms of the diagram that the baby girl in the book has a Mum and is a Mum herself. Use the illustrations in the book to show this again, if the children are unsure. How would this work with a boy baby? Explain that as a baby, he would have a Dad, but then eventually he could become a Dad himself. (According to achievement level, you could expand this to a girl having a Dad, but the Dad to her own baby would probably be her husband; a boy has a Mum, but the Mum to his own baby would probably be his wife.) What does a Mum become when her grown-up child has a baby? What does a Dad become when his grown-up child has a baby?

- Spend some time talking about the children's own families. Ask the children why our brothers and sisters are our brothers and sisters. Do any of them have grandparents? Do they know what grandparents are? Can they say whose Mum and/or Dad their own grandparents are? Do they have uncles and aunts? How do these people fit in? Explain that uncles and aunts are their parents' brothers and sisters. What will their brothers and sisters become when they have their own children? What will they be when their brothers and sisters have children? Can anyone tell you what we call the children of brothers and sisters? (Cousins.) Do any of the children have cousins themselves? Can they tell you who the cousins' parents are and how they're related to them?

- Look at some of the photos brought in by the children and spend some time talking about the relationships. Looking at one child's photos at a time, use Blu-tack to fix them onto the flip chart in the form of a family tree (see Figure 8.2). Ask the children to help you put the photos of each generation in the right places. Let the child write under the photos the names of the different family members. Do this for two or three of the children until they understand the point you're making. Tell the rest of the children they'll all have the chance later to make their own family tree using their photos.

- Show *My Family Tree Book* to the children and discuss the first stage of a family tree (*All about me*, on page 4) and how this is similar to the trees that you have just made on the flip chart. Decide how extended you want to make the family trees and share the relevant sections of the book. Tell the children you will leave the book out for them to look at and use for ideas and support as they make their own family trees.

Focus activities

Group A:　Ask the children to draw or paint several portraits of themselves at different stages of their development. They can look at the early stages featured in *Once There Were Giants* to remind themselves. They should write a label, caption and/or sentence(s) for each of their pictures. Display their portraits in a horizontal line so that the other children can see the chronological progress of their friends' development.

Group B:　Let the children make zigzag books of *My Family*. Each page of the book should feature a member of the children's immediate family, starting with themselves. Help them to plan beforehand how they are going to make their books. They should make a list of who will feature in their books and also make a list of the materials they will need. According to achievement level, they could also complete a conventional family tree using the template of a family tree (Photocopiable Sheet 20). Leave the zigzag books and/or the accompanying family trees for all the children to explore freely.

Group C:　Let the children explore the commercially produced *Happy Families* cards, so they can design a pack of their own. Help them to plan, design and make their version of *Happy Families* featuring their own families. When the cards are ready, have fun playing the game. Encourage the children to explain to the others how to play. According to achievement level, they could write some instructions for playing the game and leave these with the cards for the other children to play freely.

Group D:　Help the children to make their own family tree with their photos, in the same way that you showed the whole group during the introductory session. (If there are any children who don't have a family, encourage them to plan a tree of a family they'd like to have, or a tree of the family in *Once There Were Giants*, as you think most appropriate.) Instead of using Blu-tack, cut slits in the sheets of card to slip the corners of the photos through. The children should label or write a caption for each photo. Ask them to highlight themselves on the tree, so that their position is obvious.

Group E: Ask the children to share their funny baby stories and also to tell about something that happened when they were in Nursery or Pre-school Group. Help them to record their stories onto a cassette and then leave the cassette player with the cassette for the other children to listen to freely.

Other structured play activities

- Ask the children to bring in several photos of themselves that show their development from babyhood to the present day. (Make sure they have permission to bring in these in.) Help them to make a display marking their growth and include labels, captions and/or sentence(s) for each photo.
- Together make a 'setting family tree', with the immediate practitioners at the parents' level, other groups' practitioners at aunts' and uncles' level, the senior management at grandparents' level and so on.
- Have a fun display of baby photos of staff members and challenge the children to guess who's who!
- If any of the children are members of a family that comes from another part of the world, use the opportunity to find out about their culture. Ask someone from their family to come in to tell and show the children about their country, culture and way of life, etc.
- Help the children to make a wall-length frieze depicting the growth of a person from baby to adult. Let them follow the stages shown in *Once There Were Giants* for support if memories need jogging. They should write labels, captions and/or sentence(s) for each stage of the frieze. An extension of this could show the developmental stages of various animals.
- Let the children play freely with the *Happy Families* cards.

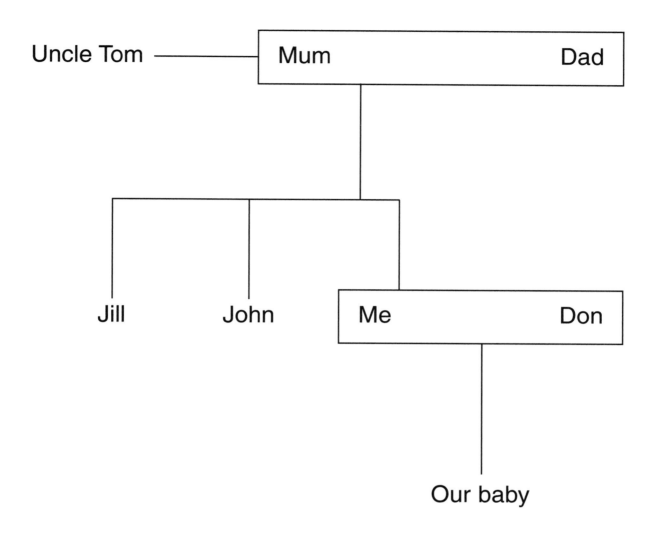

Figure 8.1 The family tree of the people in *Once There Were Giants*

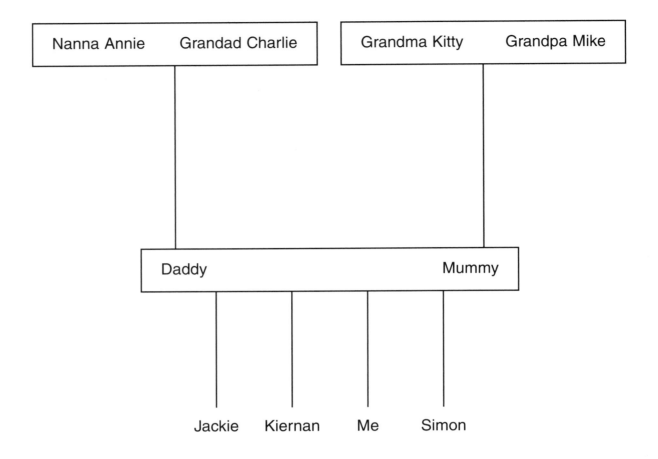

Figure 8.2 My Family Tree

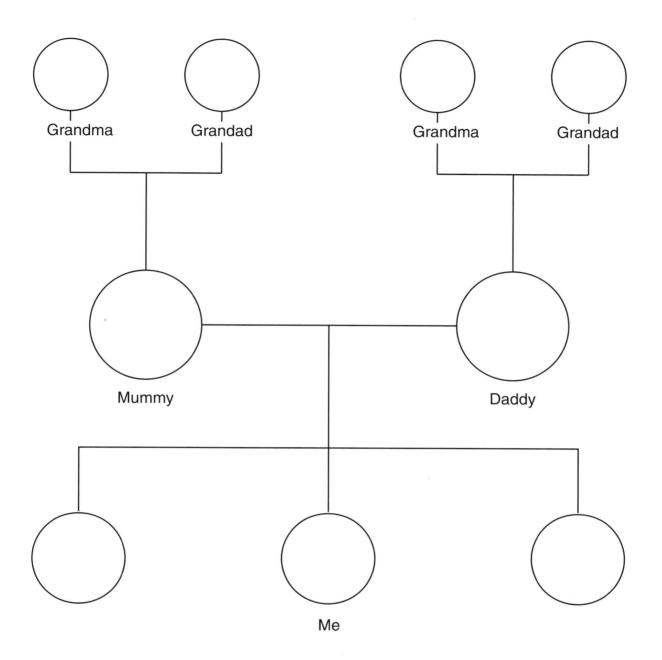

CHAPTER 9

Travel and Transport Then and Now

by Alastair Smith (Usborne Publishing 2000)

Text synopsis

The book has cartoon-type illustrations and information in 'bite-size' chunks, and follows the development of different types of transport, from cavemen who walked to get to their destination, to all the modes of travel that the children are familiar with today. You can pitch the discussion to suit the achievement level of your children, going into as much or as little detail as you think appropriate.

Early learning goals from *Curriculum guidance for the foundation stage,* Communication, language and literacy:

- Sustain attentive listening, responding to what they have heard by relevant comments, questions or actions.
- Use talk to organise, sequence and clarify thinking, ideas, feelings and events.
- Show...how information can be found in non-fiction texts to answer questions about where, who, why and how.

Objectives from the *National Literacy Strategy (YR)*:

- To make collections of personal interest or significant words and words linked to particular topics.
- To think about and discuss what they intend to write ahead of writing it.

Objectives from the *National Literacy Strategy (Y1)*:

- To predict what a given book might be about from a brief look at both front and back covers, including blurb, title, illustration; to discuss what it might tell in advance of reading and check to see if it does.
- To write labels for drawings and diagrams.
- To produce extended captions, e.g. to explain paintings in wall displays or to describe artefacts.

Objectives from the *National Literacy Strategy (Y2)*:

- To read simple written instructions in the classroom . . . for constructing something.
- To learn new words from reading linked to particular topics; to build individual collections of personal interest or significant words.
- To use diagrams in instructions, e.g. drawing and labelling diagrams as part of a set of instructions.

Because very young children find the concept of time difficult, you may have to put some of the historical information in the general context of 'long ago'. Try to relate the information you share with the children to similar experiences within their own lives. When discussing different aspects of travel and transport, encourage them to think of the same aspects in their own lives. So, for example when you are looking at the early bicycles, the children can describe their own bikes; when you explore the first steam train, the children can talk about their trip on a train to go on holiday.

Materials needed

- *Travel and Transport Then and Now* by Alastair Smith (Usborne Publishing 2000), flip chart and marker pens
- Traffic census forms (see 'Preparation'), clipboards, pencils
- Sticks, paper, card, cork, etc. to make rafts and boats, scissors, glue, string
- Templates of paper aeroplanes (see 'Preparation'), coloured marker pens; cardboard, round sticks, lollipop sticks, rubber bands, junk for model cars, paint and paintbrushes, pebbles and stones (tiny, small and large) for model of Roman road, cardboard, tray or box

Optional materials for other activities

- The toy vehicles in the setting, waxed paper or card, balloons, canisters to fill the balloons, postcards, string, pens, large construction blocks, dressing-up clothes

Preparation

▲ Make enough copies of the traffic census form (Photocopiable Sheet 21 on p. 81) for each child in Group A.

▲ Use Photocopiable Sheet 22 (p. 82) to make templates of paper aeroplanes for Group C.

Introducing the text

- Look at the cover with the children and spend a few moments discussing what the book might be about. Do they know what *transport* means? If not, can they work it out from the 'blurb' and the illustration on the cover? Read the first section (*Early days*) inviting the children to read some of the text and/or the speech bubbles. Are there any words that the children aren't sure about? For example, *invented, vehicles, soar* or *transport*. Help the children use the context and illustrations to work out the meanings of any new words. Before you open the flap, spend some time with the children talking about the man from long ago who had to travel on foot. What is he dressed in? Why? What is his footwear made of? Why is he saying 'My feet are sore'? Invite one of the children to open the flap. How is the man in the picture different from the first man? What is this man dressed in?

Why? Discuss the different methods of transport inside the flap. Are there any that the children haven't seen before? For example, the cable car or the snowmobile. Explain that these are both ways of travelling that are used in countries with very high mountains where there aren't any roads. Share the rest of book with the children, taking time to explore each section. Encourage them to predict what they'll discover underneath the flap on each page, and then invite different children to lift the flaps.

- Explore the text in more detail. Are there any words that the children aren't sure about? For example, *boggy, fuel, carriages* and *propellers*. Because each section of the book explains the meanings of these words in both pictures and text, take time to discuss it thoroughly and make sure the children grasp the meanings. Invite different children to come out and role-play the cartoon sketches from each section. For example, when the men are riding the 'bone-shaker' bicycles, when the navvies are laying the railroad, when the man with experimental wings fails to fly or when the Roman legion is marching along the road. When you have finished reading, ask the children whether they enjoyed the book. Encourage them to tell you why or why not. Was there a part they really liked? Why? Was there a part they didn't like very much? Why not?

- Let the children take time to examine the illustrations in detail. Invite them to explain to you the think bubbles and the speech bubbles that some of the characters have. For example, why is the horse on page 12 saying 'Yikes! That noise scared me!' or why does the person in the steam train on page 8 say 'Oh no! It's raining'? Are there any illustrations in the book that the children find funny? For example, on page 7, the man shouting back to his companions, 'We'll be at the top in a few hours', or the picture on page 4 which shows people using logs as early 'boats'. Discuss with the children the ways that the illustrations show the contrasts between modern transport and the early versions of the same thing. Spend time exploring the differences in detail encouraging the children to look carefully and spot the changes over the years.

- What forms of transport have the children experienced themselves? On the flip chart write a list of the vehicles they have travelled on. Among their suggestions might be car, bicycle and/or tricycle, scooter, motorbike, aeroplane, ship or ferry, boat or yacht, train and bus or coach. Later you and the children could make a bar chart or graph to find the most frequently used method of transport.

Focus activities

Group A: Give the children their census forms, pencils and clipboards, and take them out to do a traffic census. Show them how to put a tick in the appropriate box when they see a certain type of vehicle. (Remind them to check the sky if they think they hear an aeroplane!) When you all come back indoors, ask the children to work out how many of each vehicle they saw by adding up the ticks. From the data they have collected, can they work out the most common form of transport in their area at that time of the day?

Group B: Using the illustration in pages 4 and 5 of *Travel and Transport Then and Now*, let the children make models of the different types of raft and boats. Encourage them to experiment with different materials such as sticks, paper or card, cork and so on, to find the ones that float most efficiently. They should write labels, captions and/or sentence(s) to go with their models. According to achievement level, they could write instructions for making the most successful of their models.

Group C: Give the children the templates of paper aeroplanes. They might like to illustrate and colour their planes before they fold them into shape. Let them fold the paper along the dotted lines to make the aeroplanes and then have fun flying them. It's probably best to do this in the hall or outside, since the aeroplanes have a nasty habit of landing where they shouldn't if they are flown in a smaller room or where there are other children. When the planes are past their 'fly by date', make a wall display with them, and ask the children to write a label or caption to go with each plane.

Group D: Let the children make some model cars using junk. (Make sure none of the children is allergic to minute traces of foods that may still be in empty packets or boxes.) They should paint the body of their car first and leave it to dry. They can then make a chassis and wheels (see Figure 9.1 on p. 80) before sticking on the main body.

Group E: Ask the children to make a model of a Roman road using the picture on page 6 of *Travel and Transport Then and Now* for support. They should collect different-sized pebbles and stones from outside and put them in layers in the box, following the size order shown in the illustration. They could make the final layer of flat slabs from cardboard painted grey or brown. Remind them to leave one end of their model road visible, showing the different layers. Ask them to write labels, captions and/or sentence(s) explaining about their model. According to achievement level, you may have to scribe for them.

Other structured play activities

- Arrange a visit to an airport observation lounge and help the children to identify the different vehicles there. Point out transport other than the aeroplanes such as the baggage trailers, fire engines, hydraulic vehicles for disabled passengers, helicopters and so on. When you come back to the setting, make a frieze of the airport and include all the vehicles spotted by the children.
- Invite the children to experiment with the vehicles in the setting. Help them to change some of the vehicles into other forms of transport. For example, they could turn a tricycle and trailer into an ambulance, a pedal-car into a ship, or a tractor into a train. Let them make up and act role-plays that involve the new methods of transport.
- Make some small boats out of waxed paper or card and have some fun with them in water play. Let the children experiment with other materials for making boats. Which are successful? Which don't float for very long? Which are strong enough to carry a little bit of 'cargo' such as a crayon?
- Go on a visit to the railway station. How many different kinds of train do the children see? Are there any goods trains? Are the wagons and bogies all the same? What other vehicles are there in the station? If possible, take the children to experience a steam train or to visit a railway museum.
- Send off some balloons with messages attached. You can get canisters to fill the balloons from good quality toyshops. Let the children write a message on a postcard and tie it firmly to the balloon – remind them to write the school address on the card if they want a reply from whoever finds it. Have a grand 'lift off' ceremony. Whose card travels the farthest?
- Involve the children in imaginative play by encouraging them to make a bus, a plane, a train and/or a boat from large construction blocks, and then to go on a journey in their mode of transport. Let them dress up for the occasion.
- Ask your local fire, ambulance and/or police service to bring one of their vehicles to the setting and explain to the children how it works and what are all the special elements to it.

Cut the wheels out of strong card and make a hole in the centre for the round sticks. Put a rubber band on each side of the wheels.

Fix a lollipop stick to the round sticks.

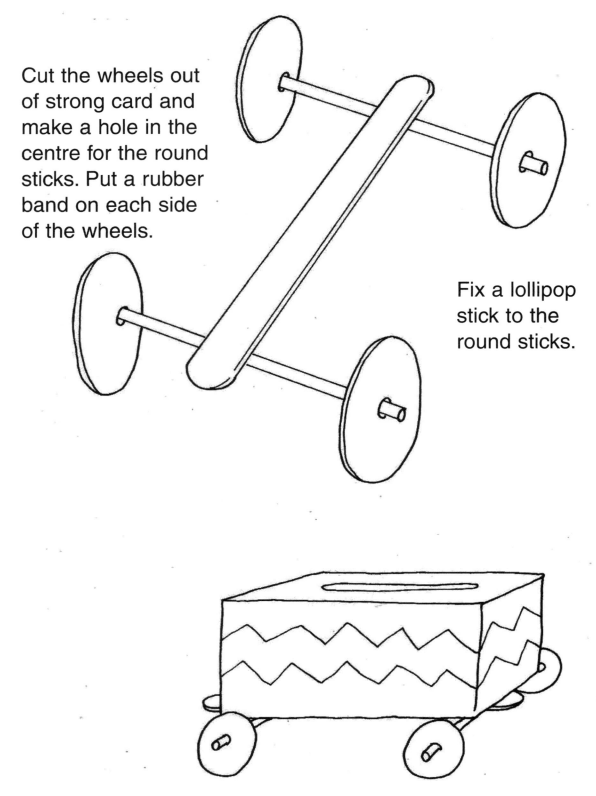

Complete the car by fixing the painted body to the chassis.

Figure 9.1 A chassis for a junk car

car				
lorry				
bus				
bicycle				
motorbike				
ambulance				
fire engine				
police car				
others				

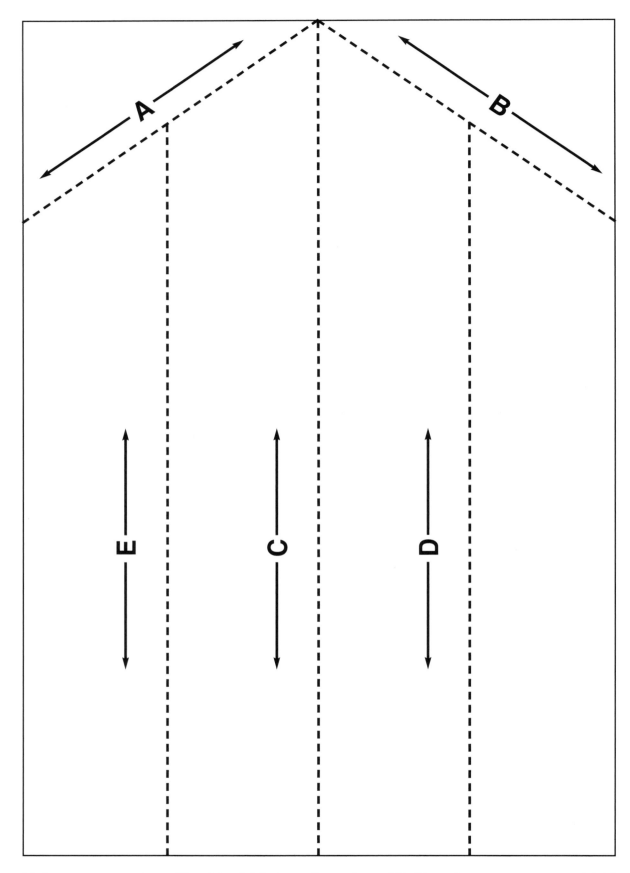

Make your aeroplane like this: fold along lines A and B. Turn the paper over and fold along lines D and E. Turn the paper back again and fold along line C. Hold your plane along the fold of line C and then send it on its way!

CHAPTER 10

Wheels Keep Turning

by Mick Manning and Brita Granström (Franklin Watts 2002)

Text synopsis

The book is illustrated with drawings and gives the information in small blocks, which makes it easy for the children to absorb. It follows the development of the wheel, from cavemen who used logs to move boulders, to all the recognisable things we have today that use wheels or the principle of turning, such as roller skates and CDs. You can pitch the discussion to suit the achievement level of your children, going into as much or as little detail as you think appropriate.

Early learning goals from *Curriculum guidance for the foundation stage*, Communication, language and literacy:

- Interact with others, negotiating plans and activities and taking turns in conversation.
- Use talk to organise, sequence and clarify thinking, ideas, feelings and events.
- Extend their vocabulary, exploring the meanings and sounds of new words.

Objectives from the *National Literacy Strategy (YR)*:

- To use knowledge of familiar texts to re-enact or retell to others, recounting the main points in the correct sequence.
- To think about and discuss what they intend to write, ahead of writing it.
- To learn new words from their reading and shared experiences.

Objectives from the *National Literacy Strategy (Y1)*:

- To learn new words from reading and shared experiences, and to make collections of personal interest or significant words and words linked to particular topics.
- To read non-fiction books and understand that the reader doesn't need to go from start to finish but selects according to what is needed.
- To write and draw simple instructions and labels for everyday classroom use, e.g. in role-play area, for equipment.

Objectives from the *National Literacy Strategy (Y2)*:

- To learn new words from reading linked to particular topics; to build individual collections of personal interest or significant words.
- To read simple instructions in the classroom, simple recipes, plans, instructions for constructing something.
- To use diagrams in instructions, e.g. drawing and labelling diagrams as part of a set of instructions.

Because very young children find the concept of time difficult, you may have to put some of the historical information in the general context of 'long ago'. Try to relate the information you share with the children to similar experiences within their own lives. When talking about different ways of using wheels, encourage them to think of how they use wheels in their own lives. So, for example when you are looking at the early wheelbarrows, the children can talk about the wheelbarrows that someone at home uses for gardening; when you explore the fairground pages, let the children share their experiences of visits to the fair.

Materials needed

- ■ *Wheels Keep Turning* by Mick Manning and Brita Granström (Franklin Watts 2002), picture of Stonehenge (optional), clockwork toy (optional)
- ■ Clipboards, pencils, paper, windmill template (see 'Preparation'), stiff paper or card, long lollipop sticks, coloured marker pens, scissors, glue, fasteners, boxes, model junk (e.g. old boxes, packets, wrappings, etc.), paints and paintbrushes, circle templates, materials to make a Ferris wheel for the wall, round sticks, stones, string

Optional materials for other activities

- ■ Materials to make a frieze of a fairground, construction kit, Photocopiable Sheet 14 (p. 55), card, scissors

Preparation

- ▲ Use Photocopiable Sheet 23 (p. 88) to prepare templates of a windmill for each child in Group B.

Introducing the text

You may choose to introduce the text over several sessions:

- Look at the cover with the children and invite them to read the title. Spend a bit of time looking at the illustration and discussing what the book might be about. Do they know what *pulleys* and *cogs* are? If not, can they work it out from the 'blurb'? Explain that they are types of wheel that help us to lift heavy loads (pulleys) or that help machinery to work properly (cogs). Look at the picture on the frontispiece. Are any of the children familiar with this? Why is the mouse in the wheel? What other pets might run around in an exercise wheel? (Hamsters, guinea pigs or gerbils.) Read the book, taking time to explore it thoroughly and inviting the children to read some of the text. Encourage them to join in the refrain *Wheels keep turning!* which appears at the beginning of each new page. Before you turn over a page, ask the children to guess what might come next.

- Explore the text and the illustrations in detail. Are there any words that the children aren't sure about? For example, *axle, chariots, stagecoaches* or *crankshafts*. Help the children use the context and illustrations to work out the meanings of any new words. When you have read the section about Stonehenge, show the picture of the ancient monument to the children and discuss with them how the stones might have been lifted upright. (If you don't have a picture of Stonehenge, spend a few moments talking about it. Does anyone know what it is? If not explain that it is a circle of huge stones in Wiltshire, put up about 4,000 years ago by people who we think might have worshipped the sun through the gaps between the stones.) Have any of the children seen a potter's wheel in action? Ask them to tell the others about it. If nobody has seen one, explain to the children how it works. Talk about the wheelbarrows invented by the Chinese – how are they different from the wheelbarrows we use today? Can anyone tell you how the pulley works? Do any of the children have something that works by a pulley at home?, such as an old-fashioned slatted dryer that hangs from the ceiling or a window blind that rolls down, i.e. not a spring-action blind? If you have anything in the setting that works by a pulley, let the children see and/or explore it. What does it mean when the text talks about wheels having *spokes*? Help the children to understand that before the Egyptians' chariots were invented, other wheels were solid. Where can the children see spokes on wheels today? For example, on their bikes, on babies' buggies or prams and on fairground wheels. Can anyone tell you what makes *cogs* special? Explain that the teeth in a cog helps it to grip another cog while it turns, which makes the other one turn as well. Has anyone ever been to a mill like the one in the picture? Invite the child to tell everyone about it. Does anyone have clockwork toys at home? If there are any in the setting, let the children explore them later at leisure, but spend a few moments now showing them how the toy works. Do the children know what a highwayman was? Are the coaches that a highwayman robbed like the coaches we ride in today? How are they different? How are the wheels different? Can anyone tell you what a farmer does when he sows, mows and threshes? Ask the children to guess how these things were done before the farmer had machinery with wheels to help him. When you read the pages about the textile mills, make sure the children don't confuse *mill* in this sense with the watermill you looked at earlier that grinds flour. Have the children ever seen cloth being woven on a loom? Ask them to tell the others about it. Do trains today still have wheels? Do cars? How are they different from the wheels of the earlier versions? Have the children ever ridden on a Big Wheel at the fair? Have they ever had a go on a roundabout? Are there any smaller roundabouts in a playground near the setting? What other roundabouts do the children know of? For example, on the roads or on entrance turnstiles. Let the children take time to look at the pictures on pages 28 and 29 of *Wheels Keep Turning*, helping them to recap on everything that the book explores.
- Finally – looking at the very last illustration in the book and the instruction that goes with it – invite someone to read what it says and then have fun doing the activity. (The book doesn't tell you the answer – I spotted the mouse 18 times, but perhaps someone will let me know if they can improve on that score!)

Focus activities

Group A: Give each child a clipboard, a sheet of paper and a pencil. Go to the street outside the setting and ask the children to spot where there are wheels. They should either draw or write the names of the things they see. Alternatively, let the children find wheels inside the setting, in the room, the hall and/or the whole building, as you think appropriate. When they have collected their data, the children should decide how they should make the information they collected available to the others. For example, by drawing pictures, drafting block graphs or by making a list.

Group B: Give the children the windmill templates (Photocopiable Sheet 23). Let them make their own windmills. They should first colour the windmill or draw a pattern on its sails before cutting it out. Then each peak should be folded gently to the centre and fastened together securely. Help the children to fix the windmill to one end of a long stick. They can make their windmills go round by blowing the sails, or by putting them outside in the wind, making sure they are firmly fastened down.

Group C: Let the children make a model train using boxes and other junk. Ask them to work together and decide on the best way to make their model. They should agree things such as the finished size (whether they are going to make a table-top model or one that is big enough to play in), the materials they are going to use, how they are going to assemble it and so on. Encourage them to experiment to see whether their ideas work, and if not, to have a rethink.

Group D: Ask the children to make a giant Ferris wheel for the wall. Let them use the illustration in *Wheels Keep Turning* if they need a model to copy. They should put capsules or seats on their wheel, filled with people. Let them draw self-portraits for the passengers. According to achievement level, challenge them to work out a way to fasten the Ferris wheel to the wall in such a way that it can be turned around. Will they have to adjust the seats if they make their wheel move?

Group E: Give the round sticks, stones and string to the children. They should work together to do an experiment that recreates the rollers that moved the stones to Stonehenge. Let them look at the pictures in *Wheels Keep Turning* to give them ideas. According to achievement level, ask them to write some instructions for how to make the rollers work, the other children can have a go at the experiment later on.

Other structured play activities

- Help the children to make a fairground frieze including as many amusements that involve wheels as possible. Ask the children to plan beforehand what attractions, amusements and stalls they want to include in the frieze. According to achievement level, challenge them to design attractions with moving wheels.
- Let the children make an axle like the one on page 6 of *Wheels Keep Turning*. They should write labels, captions and/or sentence(s) to go with their models. According to achievement level, they could write an account of how they made their axles, or, alternatively, they could write some instructions for the other children to make one.
- Leave *Wheels Keep Turning* in the Book Corner for the children to explore in their own time. Remind them that they can have fun looking for the little mouse on each page.
- Give the children Photocopiable Sheet 14 (p. 55) to make spinners. Ask them to colour the sections before they thread the string through the holes. Let them have fun playing with their spinners.
- Give a construction kit to the children and encourage them to make a pulley. They could look at the picture of a pulley in *Wheels Keep Turning* to get an idea of how to put the various parts together. Encourage them to try out their pulley with a small weight. According to achievement level, you may have to give the children a bit of help.

- Let the children make a spinning top (see Figure 3.3 on p. 81 of *Literacy Play for the Early Years* Book 4: *Learning through phonics*) and have fun making up different games by putting a variety of things in the spinning top's sections. For example, it can be used to score in games by having numbers written on the sections; or it can be used to play a form of *Spin the Bottle*, by having instructions such as *Sing a song, Say a nursery rhyme* or *Tell a joke* written on the sections.
- Visit a mill – either a windmill, a watermill or a textile mill – and let the children see how the cogs, wheels and pulleys make the machinery work.

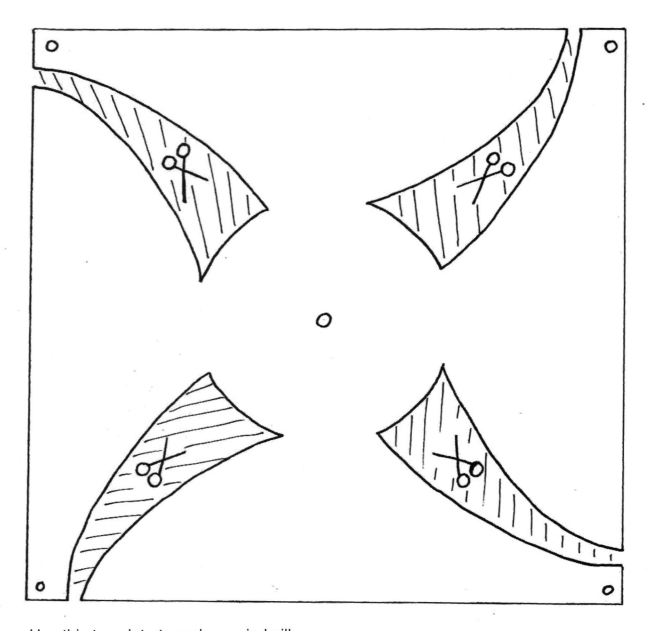

Use this template to make a windmill.

Observation and assessment for speaking and listening

During the sessions observing the children, you may find it useful to refer to some of these questions as a way of focusing on how their speaking and listening skills are developing:

- Do all the children make a contribution to the whole-group or small-group discussion?
- Are the grammatical structures correct? Is the syntax correct?
- Do the children use appropriate vocabulary? Do they use context to work out unfamiliar words?
- Do the children show a curiosity about new words and try to explore how to use them appropriately?
- Is their speech fluent and clear?
- Do the children sustain attention when listening?
- Do the children listen with respect to others' views and opinions?
- Do the children take turns in conversations?
- Do they appear to understand what is being said by you and by the other children?
- Do the children ask relevant and appropriate questions about a shared text?
- Do the children have a concept of the sequence of a story?
- Do the children use the illustrations for clues about the meaning, sequence and content of the story?
- Do the children talk about key events and characters in a familiar story?
- Are they able to negotiate plans and roles?
- Do they enjoy listening to stories, rhymes and songs, and are they able to respond to them, taking part and using them in their play and learning?
- Do the children use language in their imaginative play? Do they role-play and create imaginary experiences?

Observation and assessment for reading and writing:

During the sessions observing the children, you may find it useful to refer to some of these questions as a way of focusing on how their reading and writing skills are developing:

- Can the children hear and say initial and final sounds in words? Can they hear and say short vowel sounds within words?
- Can the children name and sound the letters of the alphabet?
- Do the children know that print in English is read from left to right, and from top to bottom?
- Do the children enjoy exploring and experimenting with sounds, words and texts?
- Do they have a knowledge of the vocabulary of literacy, such as 'book', 'cover', 'page', 'line', 'title', 'author', 'front', 'back', 'word', 'reading', 'writing', etc.?
- Can the children write their own name?
- Do they attempt to write for different purposes, such as letters, lists, instructions, stories etc.?
- Do the children use their knowledge of phonics to attempt to read or write simple regular words?
- Can they hold and use a pencil appropriately?
- Do they write letters using the correct sequence of movements?
- Can the children recognise the important elements of words such as shape, length and common spelling patterns?
- Do the children use different cues when reading, e.g. their knowledge of a story, context, illustrations, syntax, etc.
- Can they identify significant parts of a text, e.g. captions, characters' names, chants, etc.?
- Are the children aware of the structure of a story, i.e. a beginning, a middle and an end? Are they aware of the actions and consequences within a story?
- Do the children check text for sense? Do they self-correct when something they read does not make sense?
- Can the children identify patterns in stories and poems? Can they extend them?
- Can the children match phonemes to graphemes? Can they write them?
- Do they understand alphabetical order?
- Can the children sight-read familiar words such as captions or high frequency words?